D0901931

STARTING POINT

Journeys of Teen Moms Who Overcame

STARTING POINT

Journeys of Teen Moms
Who Overcame

Stories compiled by

TIFFANY STADLER

Illustrations by
Madison & Mackenzie
Stadler

REDEMPTION
PRESS

© 2016 by Tiffany Stadler. All rights reserved.

Published by Redemption Press, PO Box 427, Enumclaw, WA 98022

Toll Free (844) 2REDEEM (273-3336)

Redemption Press is honored to present this title in partnership with the author. The views expressed or implied in this work are those of the author. Redemption Press provides our imprint seal representing design excellence, creative content, and high quality production.

No part of this publication may be reproduced, stored in a retrieval system, or transmitted in any way by any means—electronic, mechanical, photocopy, recording, or otherwise—without the prior permission of the copyright holder, except as provided by USA copyright law.

All Scripture quotations, unless otherwise indicated, are taken from the *New King James Version*. Copyright © 1982 by Thomas Nelson, Inc. Used by permission. All rights reserved.

Scripture quotations marked NIV are taken from the *Holy Bible, New International Version*®. *NIV©*. Copyright © 1973, 1978, 1984 by International Bible Society. Used by permission of Zondervan. All rights reserved.

Scripture quotations marked MSG are taken from *The Message*. Copyright © 1993, 1994, 1995, 1996, 2000, 2001, 2002. Used by permission of NavPress Publishing Group.

Cover design by Brittany Osborn, Nathaneal Clanton, Madison Stadler, and Mackenzie Stadler.

ISBN 13: 978-1-68314-156-3 (Print)

Library of Congress Catalog Card Number: 2016959817

MY PRAYERFUL NOTE TO YOU...

TO:_____

FROM: _____

I BOUGHT THIS book for you, and it was meant to be placed in your hands. It may be to simply pass through you and become a blessing to someone else. It may be that it was meant to be placed in your hands on this exact day for this exact moment.

May this book give you hope.

May this book encourage you. Empower you. Inspire you.

May this book change your life.

May it be your own personal *starting point*.

MY HEART BEHIND THIS BOOK...

DEAR TEEN MOM (or soon-to-be Teen Mom),

This book is for you.

This book is also for every educator who works with kids in tough situations, for church leaders, for parents, for anyone who wants to understand the heart of a hurting youth.

This book is for you.

Many of the stories may be tough to read. Behind the words is a lot of hurt. Many of these women have been through tough stuff. Some of their stories will walk you through a short season of their lives, and others will take you down the road of a rocky several years' journey.

You will walk with them through the early life events that led to teen pregnancy, and hear the different reactions to a positive pregnancy test.

You may even hold your breath with them as they climb over boulders that seem impossible, while they continue on their path towards a better future.

You may connect with many of them as they go through a roller-coaster of emotions—from hurt, excitement, and anger, to joy. You will understand through these stories how being a teen mom changes your entire life, as do the decisions made along the way.

You are not alone!

You will also be part of each woman's journey as they choose to let a God they didn't know, a God who was there when they didn't know it, come in and radically change their lives.

Please be reminded that these are *their* stories. When you are reading, and see the name God or Jesus, and it freaks you out, or maybe you don't believe, please continue to read on.

Why? Because these stories are meant to encourage you. They may even transform your life as you read and connect with women who have been in your shoes.

Being a teen mom, or a mom at any age, is not easy. I applaud you for opening this book, because it is a step towards fighting for a better future for you and your baby. Continue to seek others who will speak encouragement into your life, and don't be afraid to ask for help. I am so excited to use my story, as well as the other women's stories, to impact and inspire the lives of other teen moms.

One thing that I have learned about God over the last several years is that *everything* is in His timing, and He will make it great! You may be in a place of feeling hopeless, weak, and discouraged. I was there too, and know how it feels; despite that, as I look back on my journey, I know that every piece of it was worth walking through. It made me stronger and it made me who I am today.

I am sure you've heard the phrase, "If He brings you to it, He will bring you through it," at some point in your life, and it is so true! God can take all things, every situation, and use it for His glory.

You are not alone!

Above all, this book was written to give you hope. There has been a tugging in my spirit for many years to sit down, get my story on paper, and gather other stories; but I kept telling myself that I didn't have time, that I am not a writer, and that I didn't have the ability to put it all together in a book.

I would tell myself that maybe I would try writing when life was less busy—but I also knew there would never be a perfect time. I reminded myself that I wasn't ready when I found out I was pregnant in high school, yet somehow found the strength to be a mom. I finally stepped out in obedience and began to write. God did the rest! He handpicked every woman who *He* wanted to share her story and placed them in my path.

To the women that shared their stories and hearts, and saw the vision for this book as a tool to impact lives...*thank you*! It's not easy to look back at what you walked through, or share with others what the "old you" looked like. To be honest, I was the last to complete my story, because it isn't easy; however, each of you pushed through because you knew that your story just might change one life, and that the struggle would be worth it. Adversity can do two things: It can either define you or refine you into who you are called to be. You ladies chose not to allow your past to define you. Your strength and courage is matchless! You are overcomers! But it takes a world changer to reach down and help others. You women are *world changers*! Each of you is such a blessing and inspiration to me and I am honored to have your stories in this book.

To everyone who helped point me in the right direction, and who helped turn blank sheets of paper into a book, and to those who helped edit, contributed financially, and gave ideas to make this book better... *thank you*!

To every reader, I pray that you are blessed by this book!

THE INVISIBLE GIRL

MY HEART RACED and I could feel the knots forming in my stomach as we pulled up to the abortion clinic. The protesters' shouts pierced my ears as they held up signs and screamed at us not to kill our baby. I already felt nauseous and now it seemed hard to even swallow.

> How had I gotten to this place, sitting in the waiting room of an abortion clinic?

As we entered the clinic, the staff were stone-faced and cold. I desperately needed someone to be kind and tell me it would be okay, but nobody there was friendly or comforting. I sat in the cold room, listening to a father and his daughter making jokes and laughing in the corner as if what everyone was doing was okay. I wondered why it seemed so easy for everyone. How had I gotten to this place, sitting in the waiting room of an abortion clinic?

Growing up, I was the middle child, and always very quiet. I often felt like no one heard me when I spoke, or even noticed I was there. For most of my life, I felt like an *invisible girl.*

When I was two years old, my mom divorced my father. He was rarely home because his priorities were drinking and partying. Eventually, my mom got fed up, and divorced him. Since I was so young, I'm sad

11

to say that I have no memories of my father living with us. My mom remarried shortly after the divorce, and my biological dad signed away his parental rights so my mom's new husband could adopt all three of us. My mother paid my dad one thousand dollars to comply with her request, and then he disappeared from our lives.

At first, it seemed the perfect fit with her new husband, my stepdad—but soon after, they had a baby together, and that little girl became the "apple of his eye." She was unable to do any wrong in his eyes. My siblings and I became a huge burden to him and I was once again *the invisible girl.*

Not long after my new sister arrived, I began to fear my stepdad intensely. He was heavily involved in drugs and stored them in my dresser. He only had to tell me once never to open the top drawer. I was terrified of him and that fear kept even a curious little girl from ever looking in the top drawer of her very own dresser until I was thirteen years old.

At the age of thirteen, one of the happiest days of my life was when my stepdad finally moved out of the house. Things were difficult for my mom, being a single parent of four kids, but she did her best. My stepdad moved to California to continue his drug sales, and we stayed in Colorado.

My stepdad decided to try to get my mom back—he wanted her to remarry him and move to California. He knew the easiest way to do it was through the kids. He started becoming overly nice to all of us. I remember thinking: *He wants me, look how he is being so nice!* I convinced myself that he had changed, and when he asked us kids to go to California to stay with him (in hopes my mother would follow), we packed up our things and said goodbye to Colorado. I hugged my mom a little tighter that day, unsure of when we would see her next.

After spending some time in California, I had a strange burning in my spirit. I couldn't explain it, but I just had to attend the private Christian school in the area. I was never religious, but for some reason this urge was unrelenting. I knew I was supposed to go, but the only problem was my stepdad was not willing to pay for any of it. My needs didn't matter to him. The fact that he was willing to pay for my sisters to attend was a slap in my face and left me feeling like *the invisible girl,* once again. But I was filled with determination and nothing was going to stop me. So at thirteen years old, I found a job at a video store. I worked from the time I got out of school each day until about 8 p.m. and every weekend. It was long hours and I was exhausted, but my desire drove me. I made $160 per month and put every penny I made towards my tuition and school needs. Although it was tough working and being a full-time student, I knew I had to be there.

It was at this school I learned about Jesus. This may be hard for some of you to understand, but during my time there, I heard God speak to me and say, "If you have sex before marriage, you will get pregnant." I wasn't scared about Him telling me this—by that time I was used to praying. I just thought to myself, "No worries, I would never do that."

Even though this stuck in my mind, I soon went against what I knew in my heart.

After we lived with my stepdad for only a year, I decided I wanted to move back to Colorado to be with my mom. The house we lived in was overrun with mice and cockroaches. His drug dealing out of the house not only continued but it worsened. The people who stopped by scared me. A friend of my dad's (a forty-eight-year-old man) even made a pass at me.

When I told my dad I wanted to move back to Colorado with my mom, he made it known he didn't want me to leave. I know he believed if he had possession of me that there was still hope for his relationship to mend with my mom.

My determination kicked in once again, and at the age of fourteen, I hitched a ride with a stranger and headed east towards Colorado. I kept thinking: *Please God, just get me back to Colorado.* It was not a fun time—I even had a severely infected toe and no one to help me. No one had any idea where I was, but I finally made it home after two weeks on the road with strangers.

I met my boyfriend the same year I moved home. He wasn't aware of my real age. I'm not proud that I lied and told him I was eighteen. He didn't know my real age until we had been going out for about a month. I always looked older than I was and I lied and told him I was in college. He was shocked to learn I wasn't even fifteen years old. He stopped seeing me for about a week after I told him this news, but I

> I was only fifteen!
> How could I be
> pregnant?

knew I wanted to be with him and kept calling him.

His parents raised him in church, and that's where we went on our very first date. I loved going to church with him, and was thrilled to learn we shared the same faith. When the school year resumed, I continued going to high school, and he moved several hours away to pursue his college degree. We would talk once a week on the phone, and he would visit on school holidays. It was hard being so far away from him.

We had only been dating about six months when I started feeling sick. My period was late, and although we used protection, we didn't use it all of the time. The words I heard God speak to me when I attended the Christian school started to ring in my ears once again.

I went to Planned Parenthood hoping to prove my suspicions wrong. It felt like someone punched me square in the gut when the test came back positive. I was only fifteen! How could I be pregnant?

Since the college my boyfriend attended was in a remote location, we were only able to talk on a scheduled day, at a scheduled time, once a week. I didn't have a phone and had to go to my aunt's house on Sunday evening to make the phone call. It was incredibly difficult waiting for that day to come! I can't remember exactly what I said during that conversation, but he got in his car and drove the five hours home that night.

When he arrived at my house, we really didn't know what to say to each other. Although I had very mixed emotions, we decided the best choice was to have an abortion. I knew in my heart I really didn't want to go through with it, but felt like it was my only option. My heart was racing when I called the clinic to make the arrangements to end my pregnancy.

On the day of the appointment, I forged a note with my mom's signature to get out of school. My boyfriend went to his grandmother and asked to borrow $200 to cover the cost of the procedure. He lied to her about what it was for—he told her it was for college expenses. He picked me up from school and we drove to the clinic in another city. That's when we pulled up and saw a lot of people picketing and protesting outside the abortion clinic. I was so frightened and I just felt sick to my stomach. It felt like I was living out of a scene from news footage that I had seen on TV.

During that time, this was a common scenario at abortion clinics—however, as a small-town girl, I had never seen this firsthand. For the first time in my life, I actually wished *I was invisible*. Sitting in the waiting room was where I finally broke down. I began to sob uncontrollably and couldn't stop. I could tell my boyfriend was feeling uneasy with the situation as well. His hands were trembling and he was fighting to hold back the tears in his eyes. At that moment, he reached over, grabbed my hand, and said, "Come on, we're leaving. We don't belong here."

As we walked out, my boyfriend noticed two of the picketers were his Sunday school teachers from when he was a little boy. The couple didn't recognize him, yet I think seeing a familiar face may have given him some comfort, assuring him he was making the right decision.

We got in the car, took a deep breath, and began to drive away. We drove about a quarter mile before I suddenly felt the car traveling very quickly in reverse towards the picketers. I was confused, and still in a state of shock, so I remained silent.

Thoughts began running through my head...*Oh no, he's changed his mind and is going to make me do it!* To my surprise, when we reached the picketers, my boyfriend rolled down the window and boldly stated, "We didn't kill our baby today. We didn't do it!" The picketers were thrilled that we had not gone through with it. I believe it gave them comfort to know that they had a part in our decision. As we drove away my boyfriend turned to me and told me that he clearly heard God speak to him saying, "I will bless you for the decision you made today. I will take care of you." We drove to his parents' house in silence, terrified at what we would face when we got there.

When we arrived at my boyfriend's home, telling his parents that his fifteen-year-old girlfriend was pregnant was one of the hardest things he ever did. His parents were very quiet. I knew they were extremely disappointed. My boyfriend's parents were ministers and he was an only child. They had high hopes he would follow their Christian example. They told him he needed to take responsibility for both this baby and for me. They told him that he needed to marry me and he reluctantly consented. I felt amazed that he was going to marry me—I really loved him, but I figured I would raise the baby by myself.

Although we were emotionally exhausted, we knew the right thing to do was to make the half-hour drive that same day to break the news to my mom. The news was difficult for her. She was also a teenager when she gave birth to my older brother and knew firsthand the difficulties we would face. She didn't know what to say, so she didn't speak to me for three days. I think she was in total shock. I knew she wasn't ignoring me because she was angry; she just felt defeated. Prior to this, she talked about the "birds and bees" with me and I lied to her saying I was not having sex. She felt confident I was telling the truth.

I didn't plan to get pregnant. But now that I was, in my distorted thinking, I thought: *Finally, I won't be invisible anymore.* I will have a husband who sees me and loves me. I will have a baby whom I can love. And he or she will love me in return.

We had to go to a judge to get special permission to be married. In our state of Colorado, if you are under the age of sixteen, your parents can't sign for you to be married. You need special permission from a judge. The judge did not want us to be married, but finally relented and we were married six weeks later in our home church. By the look on the faces of everyone in our wedding pictures, you could tell they were thinking we would never make it.

Our daughter was born on Christmas morning, and she was beautiful, soft, and pink. Because I was so young, I almost felt like I was playing pretend. That didn't last long. Babies are hard work! It was nothing like when I played house with dolls as a little girl.

Being teen parents took a huge toll on us, even though our parents helped us as much as they could. We lived in low-income housing and were on state assistance for food because we only made $42 per week with my job. My husband began partying a lot as a way to cover his feelings of being trapped in our marriage. He became an alcoholic, and I knew I couldn't let my daughter live the same kind of life my father created for me with his drugs and alcohol abuse. While my husband was away one day, I packed up our belongings, moved out of our apartment, moved back to my mom's house, and filed for divorce.

Coming home to an empty apartment was a wake-up call for him. Since he was raised in a Christian home, he knew where to go for help. He fell on his knees right then and gave his life back to Christ. I continued with the divorce and after three months, it still was not finalized. He was fighting me for joint custody of our daughter. During this time, I began to see a difference in him and my heart began to soften as he tried to prove to me he'd changed. The fact was, we still loved each other, and so we decided to give our marriage another try.

I wish I could say things are perfect now and we have been living "happily ever after." I can't. What I can say is after twenty-eight years, I am still married to my best friend and the love of my life. We have three children; our Christmas blessing little girl and two truly amazing sons.

When I look at the woman our daughter is today, I could not be a prouder mama. She is married to a wonderful man, and is a mother to two precious girls. Which means I get be grandma, or "Grammy" as they call me. I can't imagine the hole that would be in my heart if I had followed through with the abortion that day and ended her life before it began. As I reflect back on my journey, I thought it was the picketers that helped change my situation that day, but I know now that it was the incredible man by my side, who was taught at a young age to listen to the voice of God in every situation to guide him. My husband's obedience and my childlike faith to follow his lead were what led us out of that clinic. Picketing and making people feel shameful for their decisions isn't what I want you to capture from my story. That's not Jesus! It was God gently, lovingly, leading us out of that clinic. He was our comforter in that difficult situation, and He is who we continue to seek to this day, allowing Him to lead us in every decision.

My life really began when I surrendered it to Jesus. I do not have an earthly father who claims me as his own, but I am the daughter of my loving heavenly Father. He knows me. He sees me. He loves me. I was not then, am not now, and will never be *the invisible girl.*

> I can't imagine the hole that would be in my heart if I had followed through with the abortion that day

See what great love the Father has lavished on us, that we should be called children of God! And that is what we are! The reason the world does not know us is that it did not know him.

—1 John 3:1 (NIV)

WALK AWAY

IT'S EASY TO get hooked on drugs when they surround you in every area of your life, and your brother and mother are the suppliers.

My mom enjoyed partying and liked having her kids partake with her. She spent most of her time drinking, smoking pot, and doing methamphetamines with my brother, so the two of them became very close. I tried so hard not to go down that path, but I wasn't strong enough to *walk away*.

I smoked my first joint in ninth grade, and loved it. It only took one time and I was hooked. Giving in was easier, going with the crowd was more fun, and I began to feel like I finally fit in.

It didn't take long for my life to spiral out of control. I was hooked on pot and experimented with methamphetamines. That led to an arrest for a hit-and-run when I was fourteen years old. My friends had a car and they would sometimes let us drive around the neighborhood. The one time I decided to give it a try I was high from smoking pot and thought I was a big shot. I went too fast and couldn't stop. I crashed the car right into a parked truck. I was so afraid that I took off running, thinking I wouldn't get in trouble. Little did I know, my friends ratted me out right when the police came. I was arrested later that same day at home.

I went to court and received four years of probation, many hours of community service, and had to pay a lot of expensive fines. My mom was extremely angry with me because the responsibility for paying those fines landed right in her lap. On top of that, she had to drive me all around town to do my community service. I hated being stuck in this destructive cycle, acting like my mom, and being in trouble with the law. Yet for some reason, I just couldn't *walk away.*

Getting arrested and being on probation didn't slow me down a bit. I met a guy while I was in the system. He was funny, had a nice build, and knew how to talk his way into a girl's heart. We went to the same high school and started to hang around the same group of people.

One night we ended up at a party together and everyone was drinking. I had way beyond my limit and so did he. He talked his sweet way to me and we ended up having sex.

That was all it took to change my entire life.

It wasn't long before I realized that something was very wrong. I felt sick and had missed my period. I didn't take a pregnancy test until about three months later, because I was so afraid of what it would say. I was living in denial, convincing myself that I couldn't possibly be pregnant after just one night. I stopped smoking pot and drinking a couple months later, just in case. I could no longer tell myself that pregnancy wasn't possible or hide my growing belly. I went to a store in town and stole a pregnancy test. I was so nervous! It didn't even take a minute and the test came back with two undeniable, solid pink lines.

At fifteen years old, I sat staring, with my heart racing, at a positive pregnancy test. At that moment, I thought my life was over.

I finally broke down and called the doctor to make an appointment. I had the guy that contributed to my pregnancy come to the doctor with me, but I made him stay in the car. I checked in at the front desk feeling very anxious. My heart raced as they led me to an exam room where I sat silent and afraid, waiting for the doctor.

When the doctor entered my room she informed me she would need to do an ultrasound to confirm the pregnancy since my last menstrual cycle was a few months back. After everything was set up, she turned the screen in my direction and with surprise in her voice said, "You're having *twins!*"

I had no idea what to say, but initially felt excited as I always thought twins would be fun. The doctor confirmed I was four months along and that both babies looked healthy. She then informed me that because I was having twins it would be considered a high-risk pregnancy, and she did not specialize in those. I would need to see a specialist at St. Vincent's Hospital in Portland, Oregon. She finished the appointment by printing off pictures of Baby A and Baby B.

I walked out of the doctor's office and went straight to the parking lot to share the news. I hardly knew this man that sat in the car, yet he was the father of my children. He glared in my direction with irritation as I made my way closer. I was scared to tell him, and could hardly get the words to come out of my mouth. I handed him the pictures and he was unsure of what they were. I pointed and showed him Baby A and then Baby B. He freaked out and left, slamming the car door behind him.

Now it was time for me to go home and break the news to my mom. We were on Section 8 housing assistance, food stamps, and I sometimes had to sleep outside so my mom could party. Poverty was all we knew. What was I going to do with two babies? How was I going to be able to afford anything or provide for them? I didn't want my kids to grow up the way my brother and I did. My mom was not the greatest parent and my father simply was not around. How was I going to finish high school and get a job?

I walked into my house and thankfully my mom wasn't home. I set the ultrasound pictures on the table and left for a few days. I knew she was not going to handle it well and I didn't want to be around when she found out.

After taking several days to calm down, the father of the twins agreed to talk and figure out what we were going to do. When I told him I planned to keep the babies, he kept his distance. He wanted me to have an abortion, and was angry when I wouldn't consider it. It seemed easy for him to just *walk away*, but I knew I couldn't.

His mother was excited about my pregnancy. She was a homemaker and enjoyed being home with kids, so I stayed close with her. She was also a drug addict, but while my mom was preoccupied partying with my brother, his mom went to all of my appointments with me and took care of me. I knew I didn't want my babies raised in a drug- and

I knew I had to grow up fast and get control of my life

alcohol-fueled environment, so I knew I had to grow up fast and get control of my life if I wanted my children to have something different.

One month after seeing the doctor for the first time, I returned to find out the gender of my babies. An ultrasound confirmed that the twins were both girls. I was beyond excited and couldn't keep it in. Their biological father was still wanting me to give them up for adoption now that termination was no longer an option. I knew I had to stand my ground! I had already made up my mind.

About five months into the pregnancy, a test came back that both my girls might have Down Syndrome. When I went in to have an amniocentesis, I saw the size of the needle and listened to the risks, and I decided not to have it done. I felt that even if there was something wrong with the girls, I'd chosen to be their mother and would follow through with it no matter what. The girls' dad and my mom both protested my decision. He didn't want to be the father of a couple of "retarded kids," he said. I mentally prepared myself to give birth to two daughters who might not be as perfect as I had planned.

I had a healthy pregnancy overall, except at the end I started to swell all over and my blood pressure was extremely high, causing toxemia. After what I thought would be a normal checkup, I was admitted into the hospital, and induced into labor. I was nervous to have the babies, and not ready to go through any of it. I was stuck with IVs all over and had three belly monitors to check for contractions and to monitor the babies' heart rates. Thankfully, I was able to rest through the night with IV pain medication.

Labor started that morning. I was between 3-4 centimeters dilated but my water hadn't broken, so they manually broke all three. Yes, *three*—one for each girl, and one around them. It was a very strange feeling having all that fluid come out of me. After that, I started feeling the contractions and requested an epidural. I was terrified and it felt like a shockwave through my back.

After thirty minutes, I was still feeling some contractions on my right side, so the anesthesiologist came back and repeated the procedure. This time it worked, I was finally at peace and able to rest. But not for long since I progressed quickly.

They took me to the operating room just in case I had to have an emergency C-section. I had Twin A, weighing 5 pounds and 19.5 inches long, and Twin B, weighing 4 pounds, 13 ounces and 19.5 inches long. They were both delivered naturally and healthy. All my fears about having Down Syndrome babies were for nothing! I was so excited to hold them after delivery—but because I'd lost so much blood, I crashed. I almost had to have a blood transfusion and received extra fluids. I woke up later that day and was finally able to hold my daughters.

Just one week after I had turned sixteen years old, I became a mommy to two of the most beautiful girls in the world. I was young and nervous, but overcome with joy. As I held them in my arms, nothing else seemed to matter. I made a promise to them that I would always be there for them, and would never *walk away*.

A few days later, we went home. I was nervous about how to take care of them without the nurses' help and being able to sleep during the day. We settled in at my mom's house and everything went well at first. Their paternal grandmother came over daily to help me feed, change diapers, rest, and clean. My mom and brother would help in the evenings when they were home. It was a lot to take in, but I had it in my mind and heart to do the best I could.

Living at my mom's house began to get harder and harder as time went by. My mom and brother were still using drugs, and having people over who used. When my girls were six months old, I knew I could no longer live at home and have them exposed to that lifestyle. I had to protect them. Although moving in with the girls' paternal grandmother was not ideal, it was better than where I was. She was very helpful and I needed it. The only downfall was her husband. He was an aggressive alcoholic who yelled a lot. So in the evenings when he was home, I'd take the girls out for walks, then a bath and put them straight to bed so we didn't have to interact with him much.

After a few months of living there, I started using meth again. I had to stay awake and get the housework, laundry, shopping, and most importantly, schoolwork completed. At the same time, I also started going to an alternative school. It was work at your own pace. The drugs made it possible for me to stay up all night and get work done ahead of schedule for weeks at a time.

While attending this school, I met a guy who liked to party and have fun. I should have told myself to *walk away*, but I didn't. At the age of seventeen, I moved in with him after only dating a short amount of time. It wasn't long before I was pregnant...again. I knew this was not what either of us needed, so we both agreed that an abortion was the best decision. We made an appointment at a clinic in Portland, Oregon. My boyfriend was with me, but had no compassion. He was more concerned that I wouldn't be able to have sex for a few weeks and requested that I take care of him first. It was obvious he didn't care about me. Having an abortion was the worst pain I had ever felt! After the procedure I told myself to be careful to not let this happen again.

Although I was still doing drugs daily, I was filled with determination to finish school. I worked fast and graduated with my high school diploma my eleventh-grade year.

While I was making some great choices in my life, other things still didn't click for me. I became pregnant again at eighteen years old...with my son. This time I made the decision for myself. Although I knew having another baby would be difficult, I knew another abortion was not an option regardless of what my boyfriend wanted. I stopped doing drugs as soon as I found out. Although I had a great job working for my boyfriend's dad's company, his family required me to quit and be a stay-at-home mom.

As soon as I had my son, the desire for change overwhelmed me once again. I knew I had to protect my kids and couldn't allow them to be surrounded by drug addicts. My son's dad became violent, and tried to control me. He controlled whether I could color or cut my hair, who I was allowed to hang out with, and even made me prove I was on my menstrual cycle, otherwise he thought I was cheating on him. He would pay people to follow me when I would leave, to see where I was going and what I was doing. He cheated on me several times with several different women. I'd cry myself to sleep each night because I was afraid of what he might do to me. Even his family would try and control me and tell me that if I didn't let him see his son they would take me to court and say false things about me. They had money and it scared me. My son's dad tried to fight for custody, planted drugs on me to make me look like an unfit parent, and I eventually had to get a restraining order against him.

I borrowed money from my aunt to hire an attorney. I had to protect my son! After months of fighting in court, I won full custody. It was proven that I was reliable, I passed all the surprise drug tests, and I had a stable living environment for my children. My ex couldn't pass all of the drug tests, so he was only granted visitation every other week. This went well for the first few months, and then he would be late or not show up. My son was devastated but I would encourage him and let him know he was loved. Eventually I learned my ex was using heroin and had found a new girlfriend. Once that happened he stopped seeing our son altogether.

I knew I had to do something different so I decided to stay with my mom and start college. My mom and brother were still using, but it was more low-key and since my brother was older he went out more and stayed at friends' houses for days at a time.

My mom became more supportive and helped when she was able, and we began rebuilding our relationship. I started working for a company cleaning apartments during the day, and received help from the state to pay for my three children to be in daycare. I decided to go to night school. This way I could work and make money during the day and my mom and brother could help watch my babies at night.

I was hungry for change! Within a year, I graduated with a degree in medical assisting. I began to feel stronger as if I was getting my life back together.

I was finally able to move out and get my own place. My girls were five years old at the time, and my son was two, so life never really slowed down. However, I was excited to have a place to call my own.

It was very stressful at times, especially after I found a job in the medical assisting field. I had to wake up early each day, get kids dropped off to daycare, and then get myself to work on time. I just told myself all day: *I can do this.* I always did my best to make sure my kids were well cared for. Since we moved to a two-bedroom apartment, my daughters were given the master bedroom to share and my son was in the smaller bedroom. I slept on the couch. I chose to stay completely away from guys for fear of repeating past destructive behaviors.

Life went on like that for about three years, and then I found a much better job. I moved back to my hometown to be closer to my mom and my aunt.

As a result of helping me with the move, my mom experienced a horrible pain in her back. She pushed it off for months, thinking she'd just pulled a muscle. She finally went to the doctor and had an x-ray, and the results were devastating! She had an egg-sized tumor on her lung, which appeared to be cancerous. The doctor decided to do a few biopsies.

When the results came back, I thought my whole world was caving in. My mom was diagnosed with stage 4 lung cancer. The doctor said they could try chemotherapy with radiation and see if it would decrease the size of the tumor. If so, they could then perform surgery.

A few months of chemo and radiation did nothing. My mom went back in and the tumor had doubled in size. She was in severe pain all day, and with the chemo medications, it just made her tired and weak. Her doctor started pain medications to help and it just got worse. The morphine made my mom hallucinate and when she realized what she said to us, she'd cry for hours.

I hated watching her suffer. She was only forty-nine. She was a heavy smoker, and it ran in my family to have lung cancer.

After six months of treatment and no improvement, my mom passed away at the age of forty-nine. The tumor grew on her pulmonary artery and it ruptured one morning while she was getting ready to shower. That day we had planned to gather the entire family at my aunt's house and spend a special day with my mom. The moment I drove into the driveway and saw the ambulance, I knew in my heart why they were there. My heart was racing as I ran to the front door. Tears flooded my eyes as I burst through the door and they informed me that my mother was gone. I dropped to the ground and hugged my children tight. The coroners put her on the stretcher in a black bag to take her away. We asked if we could say our goodbyes. They left the bag open so we could see her face. I kissed her for the last time.

After my mom died, I began using again. I took her pain medications that were left over as a way to cope. It was the only way I knew how to deal with the pain. I had already lost my dad a few years prior when he was brutally murdered. I felt as if I had no one. I became overwhelmed and depressed. I hated God and blamed Him for where I was and for taking my mom from me. I hit rock bottom.

I was taking more than ten Vicodin pills per day and calling in false prescriptions to continue feeding my addiction. Amazingly, I was still able to care for my kids even when I was high. And of course, I eventually got caught. I not only lost my job, but also ended up with twelve felony counts of tampering with drug records and mandatory classes at an outpatient program called Better Choices. By completing all the classes I had the opportunity to have all charges removed from my record.

I began my year-long rehab program with my kids in tow. I was determined to try once again to turn my life around and I had no other option but to bring them with me. It was so difficult to explain to my innocent babies why mommy had to be there. I was just grateful that I was not required to do jail time. I attended AA three times per week, group two times a week, still had to work, and had to continue caring for my kids. Life felt crazy and hopeless! But I wasn't willing to give up.

Two years later, all the charges were dropped. I had finished the program with no relapses, missed classes, or missed court dates. I was so relieved! I never lost my kids, and I was clean once again. I was determined to change my life for good this time.

I met my husband-to-be after we were set up by a friend. I was reluctant to meet him, so I kept my walls up. I was searching for something that might be wrong with him. I was shocked that he was a good man and loved God. He seemed too perfect, so I continued to search for his flaws.

Shortly after we met, he was deployed to Iraq for a year and he took my heart with him. He asked me to marry him right before he deployed. I said, "Yes." I met his family while he was gone and got to know how wonderful they are. They

> Life felt crazy and hopeless! But I wasn't willing to give up.

were nothing like my family. When he came home, we started attending church, and we were married. Church was hard for me, as I was still angry about losing my mom and dad. However, I grew close to a woman I met there and to this day, I call her my mom. I didn't feel like I could trust God, but I trusted her. Church started to feel like an okay place as my heart began to slowly soften.

I finally got to know what it felt like to have a true family. Not only was there a man in my life who loved me, but he loved my children too. We accepted him with open arms and felt blessed in our new life. As a single mom with three children, I had spent a lot of time alone at home. Our life now is so different than it was growing up. We gather as a family and go on camping trips, play at the river, hike, fish, and find joy as we grow together. We eventually welcomed another beautiful baby girl into our lives and she completed our family. My husband also has a son the same age as my son, so together we have five incredible children.

Over the last couple years, my daughters' biological father began to reach out to them. When I received his first letter, it turned my stomach. He was still in prison for theft, drugs, and firearms at that time and had over a year left of his sentence. He hadn't been around for fifteen years and now he wanted to develop a relationship with them. I set boundaries, let him know that my girls had a father now and that he would never be known as anything more than their friend. They began to get to know him through letters. It was funny to read the questions he would ask. "What's your favorite color, song, food?" and such things. But it became a new adventure for them. I talked with him on the phone and really encouraged a better lifestyle if he wanted to meet the girls in person.

He agreed to the boundaries, finished his time in prison, and has recently started to build a strong relationship with the girls. It is amazing to see how they interact with each other and talk. My girls are enjoying having him in their lives, and I am very hopeful he can stay out of trouble.

As for my son's dad, he never got his life in order. He is still using drugs and can't hold down a job. My son is happy to call my husband his dad and enjoys the time they spend together.

I've always been very honest with my kids about what I've walked through and the challenges because of it. I let drugs control my life. They numbed the pain when I couldn't handle it. Through this journey, we have all grown stronger and they have learned the true meaning of grace and love. I no longer blame God, but praise Him for what He has brought me through. He placed a man in my life who guided me to church, a safe place where I can heal and begin to allow my walls to be broken down. I am learning that God is an amazing Father, an incredible King who will never *walk away*!

> I no longer blame God, but praise Him for what He has brought me through.

The Lord himself goes before you and will be with you; he will never leave you nor forsake you. Do not be afraid; do not be discouraged.
—Deuteronomy 31:8 (NIV)

EVERYTHING WILL BE OKAY

I WAS ONLY sixteen years old when I found out I was pregnant.

My boyfriend and I had been together for a year. He was nineteen and going to school at the same community college where I was completing all of my high school classes.

One day while at school I knew something was different. I started to feel a lot of cramping, and started to worry. Although we used protection while having sex, we didn't every time. I found my boyfriend passing in the hallway and told him how I was feeling, that my period was late, and that we should probably take a pregnancy test.

We stopped by the store on our way home from school and then went to his parents' house. My heart was racing as we waited for the test to tell us the results. My heart dropped when the digital test results showed pregnant.

We sat for a few seconds just staring at each other. Finally, he hugged me and told me, *"Everything will be okay."* His words comforted me for about a minute, until my mind started taking over. How could I possibly have a baby? What would my family say? How could I tell my parents? My sister was seventeen when she found out she was pregnant. She went through so many struggles and so much pain. I saw my parents and brother go through similar hurts watching my sister struggle. How could I take my family through this journey of teen pregnancy all over again?

I felt a boldness rise up inside of me as I realized that I was going to face my consequences head on.

And how could I have been so stupid to do the same thing at an even younger age?

I told my friends about my pregnancy. I started to feel excitement when they expressed how happy they were for us. I saw other pregnant girls walking down the hallway, and they looked so cute with their big bellies.

Though I felt short bursts of joy, my mind also felt like a battlefield knowing abortion was an option and seemed so much easier. At this point, no matter what I decided, my life was going to change forever. If I kept the baby, my boyfriend's life would change, and so would my parents'. Negative thoughts began flooding my mind and I began to believe that things could go back to how they were if I ended this pregnancy. Then I could continue enjoying my teen years without a baby to deal with.

However, when I really started to think about killing my baby, I knew I couldn't do it. My head hurt even trying to think about the word *abortion*. I was shocked when my boyfriend came to me a couple of days later and said, "So are you sure you want to keep it?"

By that time, I'd already made up my mind, so his question made me feel sick and angry. I turned to him and said, "Yes, I am sure I want to keep this baby. You don't have to help me. My family will be there and support me." I never took the easy way in any area of my life. I made the choice to have sex and I knew pregnancy could be the result. I felt a boldness rise up inside of me as I realized that I was going to face my consequences head on.

Reality began to set in later, and I started to realize that the excitement I felt wasn't excitement for the situation, but it was hope. Everything wasn't going to be easy, but *everything was going to be okay.*

Soon, though, the small feeling of hope began to fade. I wondered if everything really would work out. My feelings turned to anger toward my boyfriend. I could tell he didn't want me to keep the baby. He wasn't ready to be a dad, just like I wasn't ready to be a mom. I wondered how he could be so stressed out. He wasn't the one who was feeling the pain.

He wasn't the one who was going to be changing physically. He wasn't the one who had to tell my parents. I was scared. I was afraid they would be disappointed and hurt.

My parents were good parents. They were always there for me, and were always a part of my education. We lived on a ministry ranch. Ever since I could remember, my dad had helped troubled youth. He helped guys who had tattoos all over, and girls who had babies at a young age. Now I was one of "those" girls!

I knew my parents would be helpful. My mom ran a daycare, and I watched my dad mentor other teen moms. I saw how well they responded when my sister had her daughter. I was mainly afraid of disappointing them.

We kept it secret from our family for about two weeks until I could come up with a way to break the news to them. I decided to tell my sister before the rest of the family. I knew she would understand since she'd been through this. Maybe she would have some good advice.

I called her and got right to the point. "I am pregnant." There was silence. Then she asked me when I was going to tell my parents. I hadn't really thought of a time, but I figured I could wait at least a couple more months before my belly would start sticking out. She told me I needed to tell them immediately so they could help me get proper care. Although this wasn't what I wanted to hear and overwhelmed me with fear, I knew she was right.

We decided to tell them together the next day. We also decided that it would be a good idea to not have my boyfriend there, especially since we were not supposed to be seeing each other at all! We had already been in trouble months prior for sneaking out of class together. My dad caught us and we had "the talk." I confessed I was already sexually active and he forbade us to continue our relationship. Needless to say, we didn't listen. So not only did I have to tell my parents I was pregnant, but I also had to tell them we had been dishonest, rebellious, and were sneaking around.

I took a deep breath and my sister asked my parents and brother to sit down in the computer room. My sister began the conversation—all I could do was cry. My heart raced as I finally found the words and told them I was still seeing my boyfriend. I could see the disappointment on their faces. I couldn't even look at them when I told them I was also pregnant. I felt shame, disgust, sadness, and guilt.

My brother got up and walked out. I got up to follow him, but my body felt weak. Then my dad embraced me and told me to calm down. I was crying so hard that I started hyperventilating. He told me to breathe slowly. I started to feel better but the crying wouldn't stop. Then I saw my mom, dad, and sister all had tears running down their faces.

For the longest minute there was silence. Then my dad said something I will never forget: "You need to calm down because every choice you make from now on affects that baby. You can't just worry about yourself anymore. A baby is always a blessing."

I calmed down. We sat there, hearts hurting, and started talking about the future.

My parents asked what my boyfriend thought and if he had told his parents. They also made it very clear that we were not going to move in together, which was a huge relief to me. I loved my boyfriend. I knew he loved me; however, I was still just a little girl and scared out of my mind.

That night I felt like I had grown a few years older. My father was wise and full of grace and brought so much peace to the storm, making me feel like *everything will be okay.*

Let me make one thing clear: I was no angel. My boyfriend was a partier. I wanted some freedom and so did he. He went out partying and dancing in clubs every night. When I found out I was pregnant, I knew he would understand and would be on standby for whenever I felt I needed to call him. The only problem was, while we were on the phone, I could hear a lot of people talking and laughing. I often heard other girls in the background and it started to cause issues between us. He felt that just because I was at home being pregnant, it didn't mean he had to be.

every choice you make from now on affects that baby.

I was alone, upset, and jealous. He was selfish and not ready for his life to change. Day after day, we argued. The fighting was exhausting!

I was sick throughout my pregnancy. For the first four months, I couldn't keep anything down. When I was up during the middle of the night, I would pick up the phone and call my boyfriend. I felt like it was my way of letting him know what I was going through, and making him part of it.

One day my mom grabbed the phone from me and said, "Let him sleep." I stopped calling him every time after that. I had so much anger built up towards him. He was able to do whatever he wanted, while I was home pregnant and sick. It just wasn't fair!

My mom drove me to the doctor on the day of my ultrasound. My boyfriend met us there. While sitting in the waiting room, I could feel the tension; there was mostly silence. We went into the room and the lab tech was excited for us. This was honestly the first time I actually felt excited, but I was too nervous to show it. The situation wasn't necessarily a happy one, so I really didn't know how to feel. I was so overwhelmed with joy when I heard the technician say three beautiful words: "It's a girl." I smiled and looked at my boyfriend—but his face looked mad and he wasn't smiling. Was he upset we were having a girl? I tried not to cry. I looked over to my mom—she was also smiling. I focused my eyes on my mom. She was the only thing holding me together at that moment.

We walked out and there was a long silence. My boyfriend kissed me and said, "Bye." I said nothing.

The car ride felt so long. I was so filled with hurt that I pretended to sleep. I knew I couldn't talk to my mom or I would burst into tears. When we finally arrived home and told the rest of the family, joy and smiles filled the room; however, I continued to fight back tears every time I thought of my boyfriend's reaction. How could he be mad that I was having a girl and not a boy?

When the conversation came up a few days later, he apologized for getting mad and admitted it was because he wanted a boy. I was still hurt, but I forgave him.

We were driving to our birthing class when he received a phone call. I heard a female voice and he hung up right away.

I asked him, "Who was that?"

He responded, "Umm, wrong number."

I knew something was up. The phone rang again. He looked at me and I told him to answer it. Once again, I could hear a female's voice. He told the girl it was the wrong number. I was instantly furious when

I heard the voice say his name. The only thing I could think of was that he was now cheating on me.

I told him that I heard everything, and he needed to tell me exactly what was going on. He explained to me that he was starting to sell drugs for a friend so that he could have money for us. I didn't believe him, so I made him call the number again and talk in front of me.

Sure enough, it was about drugs. My anger turned to hurt. I knew I could not let myself or my baby be around this. I could hear my dad's voice in my head reminding me about the decisions I made now affecting my baby. I told my boyfriend either he was done selling, or we were done as a couple.

Thankfully, he hadn't gotten heavily involved in it and really didn't enjoy doing it, so he decided to stop. It was a long ride to class that day!

It was the beginning of May and I only had one month to go before I graduated from high school. I was still living with my parents when we moved an hour away from my school and boyfriend. I drove back and forth every day.

We had a day off of school and I was starting to feel a little weird. I decided to call my midwife and went in for a checkup. When I saw her she looked at me a little panicked and told me I was in labor and needed to drive to the hospital right away.

I was only thirty-four weeks along. I called my parents and got their voicemail, so I left them a message. Then I called my boyfriend. My mom called back and said she was on her way. Everyone was an hour away. I was scared and alone.

Thankfully I was too early to deliver, so I was put on hospital bed rest for the next two weeks. It was horrible. I had final exams I had to study for, and was not in the mood. My family and my boyfriend were right by my side every minute. I loved having the support from all of them, but it created so much tension. I remember I would cry some days because I was in the middle. I wanted to defend both sides, but I was so mad at them too. So I would just stay quiet.

One day at the hospital, a woman stopped by and asked me: "How old are you?" "I just turned seventeen," I said. "The father of the baby is nineteen, correct?" she said.

My heart skipped a beat. I didn't like where this was going. I realized she was someone who had the authority to put my boyfriend in jail. She started asking very specific questions. I learned that if we were a couple of months further apart in age, the state would have automatically pressed charges against my boyfriend, and he could have done jail time. Then this woman started talking to my mom. I started worrying. Would she come back and report us?

Thankfully, that was the last I saw of that woman.

Thirty-six weeks was the magic number. I couldn't take it any longer. I was in physical pain, emotional pain, and completely stressed out. One of my teachers at school wanted to flunk me since I wasn't able to attend the final. The fight my mom gave the college was amazing. I could always count on her to be there for me.

Another source of support was my midwife. My midwife knew everything that was going on. She would often ask everyone to leave the room so I could tell her anything without having to worry about anyone hearing. I loved it.

At thirty-six weeks, she decided the baby would be healthy, and we continued with labor.

I decided I wanted to do labor naturally. I was fine up until the end, but by then it was too late to change my mind and get an epidural. I had a healthy baby girl with my family and boyfriend by my side. It was a magical night. I remember seeing everyone's faces covered with tears of joy. I specifically remember seeing my boyfriend break down crying after just looking at his daughter and falling instantly in love.

I started to feel a sense of relief that *everything would be okay.*

We had already picked out and agreed upon her first name; however, it was the *last* name that tended to start arguments. Obviously, my boyfriend wanted his last name and my parents wanted me to put mine. Ultimately, I knew the final decision was up to me. As I wrote down his last name on the birth certificate, I hoped it was the right decision.

When we left the hospital, my boyfriend drove us home. I was so in love with my daughter. I made a promise to her that I would never let anyone or anything hurt her...ever!

Reality started hitting all of us fast. I had graduation in two weeks. This was a huge accomplishment for me because in my mind it meant

> Realizing you need help does not make you weak. And trying to convince yourself you can do everything does not make you strong.

I had succeeded. It may not have been smooth, but I had done it.

After graduation, and once fall quarter started, I decided to continue college to get my Associates of Arts degree. Through sleepless nights, happy days, sad days, and arguments with my boyfriend, I kept fighting for a better future. I had my precious baby, and that made everything worth it. I continued to stay with my parents and still carried a lot of anger toward my boyfriend for not understanding what I had gone through. He'd visit on weekends and days off, but I still cared for our daughter mostly on my own.

Being a young mom was tough. But I think being judged by people was the hardest part.

The look of disgust people gave me when they'd see my baby and me at the store made me feel inferior and embarrassed. People would act irritated when I would use my WIC checks or my State Medical coupon. I could feel their eyes staring at me and judging me.

My boyfriend didn't have to walk through that, which continued my cycle of anger. As months went by, I started feeling less and less of anything. I started becoming cold. I thought the only way to continue raising my daughter was to ignore everyone else. I had to learn to ignore the comments of other family members, friends, and strangers.

While I thought this was the right thing, I soon realized it was hurting me more than anyone. The truth is that there is nothing wrong with letting people help. I had it in my mind that I didn't need anyone—but the truth was:

I did.

Realizing you need help does not make you weak. And trying to convince yourself you can do everything does not make you strong. This was not an easy lesson to learn and it took a long time to sink in.

I had to fight to keep the world from taking me down, and to continue living out my dreams.

I got a job and continued living with my parents, but felt like I was on this journey as a single, working mom. It was definitely hard at times, but it made me stronger. The following year I graduated with my AA degree. My daughter had just turned one. I continued down the path of working towards a better future for us. This meant my dream job of becoming an FBI agent was put on hold, but that didn't make me a failure.

My boyfriend moved in with us after our daughter's second birthday. I thought it was going to be a happily-ever-after story, but I was very wrong. I didn't realize how I'd have to start thinking about him, too. I was so used to taking care of our daughter and myself that I'd forget to include him in my plans. We had to figure out how to live with each other and still be happy.

We still loved each other, and that's what helped us every day. We also had to include my parents in this because we were living with them. I felt like we were all in a big puzzle and the pieces never seemed to fit perfectly together.

We got married when our daughter was three. We moved into a little duplex and began our journey as a family. There were ups and downs, but all of them made us better people and a better couple.

Over the years I realized I had a lot of healing and forgiveness to do. I had built up so many walls in hopes of keeping people away so I wouldn't have hurt feelings. Unfortunately, I had many adults or "authority" figures that would try to tell me what I was supposed to do. Some I listened to and from others I immediately felt judgment. I categorized most people into "They are only judging me and don't really care," which in turn caused me to become very bitter. Along the way, I realized how hurtful I could be. It caused problems in my marriage because I wouldn't let my husband tell me what to do. It caused problems in my workplace because I didn't want *anyone* to tell me what I should or shouldn't do. It was shame I felt and hadn't really let go of. I had to learn to break down those walls I had built up and let God heal my heart and hurt. It wasn't easy. It required a lot of forgiveness from me to other people, and mostly to myself. This wasn't a one-day event for me; it was a long journey! However, allowing God to work in me has brought a peace I never thought was possible.

I had to learn to break down those walls I had built up and let God heal my heart and hurt.

We now have five kids—three daughters and two sons. Who we are today is a total transformation from who we were when we started our journey, because we chose to take the steps necessary to change and grow.

We've kept a few of our friends from high school. We also have many new friendships with amazing people who have taught us so much. We put our faith in God and became closer with each other through it.

Now we are starting leadership in our awesome church and have surrounded ourselves with people who speak life into us and challenge us constantly to be better. We have been radically transformed by the people whom we have chosen to be around. They show us what a healthy marriage looks like, how to be parents, and simply love us. My parents love my husband as their own son. He looks up to them, honors them, and loves them.

Allowing God to move in our lives has blessed us in so many ways. We're not perfect, and still have a long way to go, but we work daily to be better in all areas of our lives. I know that anything is possible, and we can overcome anything. If someone had told me when I was sixteen that my life would have turned out like this, I wouldn't have believed them. I never thought I was worthy of having a life like this, or to be loved like this.

God knew how my life was going to turn out, and I chose to surrender everything to Him. I have been able to walk out what it means to forgive. I've learned to love deeply, have grace, and watch my family grow in God's truths. I wouldn't change a thing! If my life had been different, then I wouldn't be able to share my journey with others, offer a young mom hope, or tell her:

Everything will be okay.

Come to me, all you who are weary and burdened, and I will give you rest. Take my yoke upon you and learn from me, for I am gentle and humble in heart, and you will find rest for your souls.
                                      Matthew 11:28-29 (NIV)

I AM WANTED

MY LIFE BEGAN at two years of age, a toddler left in an open market on the streets of Korea.

Until then, there was no record of my existence. No one knows where I'd been those two years, whom I'd been with, or even how I ended up in that market. Where were my parents? And what events led to me being abandoned there?

These questions have haunted me my whole life. They're concerns I will never get answers to, but I have spent my entire life trying. When you start your life abandoned, it's hard not to believe everyone will abandon you at some point.

I was left to walk through life with a mountain of unknowns, desperate to know if *I am wanted.*

I was found by a police officer and three days later taken to an orphanage. It's unclear how long I was actually there. My mom told me I was there for two days and my dad says it was months. I was too young to remember. Once found, I was given a whole new identity—not that I had much of one at two years old, anyway. I was given a new name, a made-up birthdate, and a birth certificate with false information on it.

Nothing about me was real.

The struggles of being adopted have haunted me my whole life. I often felt like I wasn't loved as much as my brothers and sister were, as if some part of me was missing. I never felt good enough for anyone else in my life. I love my adopted mom more than anything, and am so grateful for the life she gave me. However, I have lived my entire life feeling incomplete.

When the two people who are supposed to love you the most, unconditionally and forever leave you to fend for yourself at such a young and helpless age, it's hard to convince yourself you're worthy of anyone's love. How could they just abandon me? If they didn't want me, then how could anyone else? Can you imagine not knowing where you came from, never knowing the true circumstances of why you were left, and never getting the answers you're looking for because they're impossible to find?

It felt as though my true identity would never be known.

After I was adopted, we continued to live in Korea until I was six. My dad had served in the military, but now both of my parents were teachers at a school on the military base. Their relationship became rocky and they eventually divorced.

My sister and I moved to Yakima, Washington, with my mom while my dad and brothers remained in Korea. After a year, my dad moved to Kettle Falls, Washington, and we were stuck in a crazy parenting mess.

For those of you who are unfamiliar with the area, the distance between Yakima and Kettle Falls is roughly 250 miles and a five-hour drive. We were supposed to live with each parent every other year and travel to the other parent's house, every other weekend. We were forced to leave friends and miss out on all our school activities. It was horrible for all of us.

Growing up was hard and I often struggled with feeling unloved and unaccepted. My parents' divorce didn't help those feelings and seemed to confirm that I was unwanted.

The year I was sent to live with my dad as part of the custody arrangement was the worst year of my life and played a major role in shaping the person I became, as well as the way I viewed life and relationships. That year my dad physically abused me just about every day. He just viewed himself as a strict disciplinarian. When I was a young girl, he forced me to sit in a corner, on my hands, for hours in "time out." Then in the third grade, he progressed to hitting me with a leather belt for wetting the bed. He made me pull my pants completely down so he could spank my bare bottom.

I lived that entire year in fear, crying in private every day, wanting to tell someone, anyone, but fearing I wouldn't be believed.

My sister stayed with my mom that year because she had just gotten braces and needed to be at her appointments and my brother was sent to a friend's house most days after school. I received my "spankings" every day when I got home from school. I often begged my brother to just come home with me, hoping he would protect me, even though he was just a kid himself. Because I couldn't bring myself to tell him what was happening, he didn't understand why I needed him to come home so badly.

I remember one Christmas Eve. We went to a Christmas party for the school. I was so happy celebrating, eating, and having fun, but mostly I was grateful I wasn't going to get hit with the belt that night, until we got home. I usually didn't cry anymore because I didn't want him to see my pain, or to know he was hurting me. But this night I sobbed, I begged and begged him not to do it. But he didn't listen—my tears meant nothing to him, and the fact that it was Christmas Eve meant even less.

After that, I tried to start hiding the evidence I wet the bed, so my dad took all of my underwear and stored them in his room. I had to ask for a clean pair every day so he would know if I peed. I lived in constant fear for that entire year. Towards the end of my required stay, my dad got a job in New Mexico. He packed up my brother's stuff and mine, dropped us off, and told my mom, "I don't ever what to see her again," pointing his finger in my direction. Again, leaving me unsure whether *I am wanted*.

I kept what happened that year a secret until my senior year of high school when my mom and family finally asked me what happened between my dad and me. They always knew something happened since I never wanted to return, but never knew the extent of it. My brothers were never abused by my dad; but my sister was often verbally abused. She was told she was fat and ugly. My dad drank a lot. To this day, my dad and I do not agree about the events which took place that year and he has never admitted what he did was wrong. As a result, we have hardly spoken in over thirteen years. I never had to stay an entire year again

My thoughts became my reality.

but still visited every other weekend and every other holiday until I was eighteen years old.

Although my family viewed me as a good kid, I spent my entire life acting out. I constantly rebelled, trying to get attention, good or bad, in any way possible. I brought cigarettes to school and got caught when they fell out of my bag during a drug awareness class, snuck out of the house after my mom and stepdad went to bed, skipped school, drank, partied, got kicked off the volleyball team for smoking pot, and ran away from home.

The lack of relationship with my dad, and the feeling of rejection from my birth parents, followed me from relationship to relationship. I wasn't able to fully trust anyone, or give my heart to anyone—yet that's just the kind of love I was so desperately seeking. I made poor relationship decisions and ran away from some really good guys because of my enormous fear of rejection. I naturally assumed they would leave me, so I left first.

When rejection came, it put me in a dark place emotionally. I battled depression so much that on numerous occasions, I tried to take my own life. I was desperately seeking someone to fill a void in my life and make me feel like *I am wanted.*

I got my first job during my sophomore year of high school at a grocery store. There was a guy there I really liked. I was willing to do anything to get his attention and for him to like me. Unfortunately, he was only interested in taking my virginity.

After that, I was in a cycle of destruction. I continued looking for love in all the wrong places, giving myself away, hoping to fill a void nothing seemed to fill. My thoughts became my reality. My mind would say *I am unwanted and unworthy of real love.*

This thought ran through my head constantly. With each relationship that ended poorly, I continued to prove myself right. I met my first official boyfriend my junior year of high school. He was a soccer star and I was a cheerleader. I was pretty sure this was what true love felt like.

However, it wasn't long before an unwanted pregnancy led me to an abortion clinic. My boyfriend was supportive, drove me there, and picked me up when the procedure was done. We had too much in our future for an unwanted pregnancy to force us to live our lives differently.

Walking through that process was a part of my life I'm not sure I have ever faced. I kept it hidden because of the fear of judgment, and the fear I would never fully heal from it. We continued with life and pretended as if nothing happened.

However, we didn't change our behavior, and soon I was pregnant again. Two bright pink lines that would change my life forever. I stared down at this pregnancy test in the bathroom of my parents' house late one school night, with my best friends beside me. I just remember laughing hysterically, then the laughing changed to hyperventilating, which eventually disintegrated into tears.

I was in shock, to say the least. Eighteen years old, in the middle of my senior year of high school, cheerleader on the cheer squad, plans for college, getting away from this town and becoming somebody great, all washed away right before my eyes over two simple, unwavering, bold pink lines.

So now the hard decisions. What do I do *this* time? Do I keep this baby or do I have another abortion? Do I just ignore the test and hope it's all a bad dream? Maybe I'd be lucky and my body would spontaneously abort on its own. Then I wouldn't have to decide. Do I give this baby up for adoption, the same as I was?

Unfortunately, nobody could make that decision for me and once everyone else found out, they would all have an opinion too.

My mom was out of town when I found out so I had a few days to try and figure out the best way to tell her, and my boyfriend, and everyone else in my life. I could just imagine the disappointment on their faces. I was always seen as the good one. Whenever anyone spoke of me, it was always with a smile. It was always about how good and respectful I was. I would never do anything bad and I would never ever get pregnant as a teenager. No, not *me!*—and all I could think about was how I was about to let everyone in my life down.

My mom, of course, flipped out. So did the rest of my family. And my already rocky relationship with my boyfriend was now worse than ever. He was in the same grade as I was, but almost a whole year younger and he saw his dreams going up in smoke along with mine. I could see the struggle in his eyes to do the right thing but I could also see all the signs of someone who wanted to just run. To run away from me, from this baby, from having to change his life and his dreams for the future.

He ultimately had to decide whether to step up and be a dad, or walk away and have no part of it. His parents wanted me to place the baby up for adoption, but I knew I could never do that after the struggles I faced being an adopted child.

I made up my mind to keep this baby.

Throughout my pregnancy our relationship went through its ups and downs. We would go through a cycle of breaking up and then making up. He would go from wanting to be a part of her life to wanting nothing to do with us. I would go through emotions of loving him and wanting him to be there for us, to hating him, and hating that his life didn't seem to be changing at all. He got to stay in school, be the captain of the soccer team, and take some other girl to prom. He got to walk at our graduation, without any consequence, without dirty looks walking down the halls, without the whispers, and without losing friendships with people who I thought would always be there for me.

As time went on, I prepared myself to raise this baby on my own.

I was determined to graduate high school, so I changed all my classes and took a double load so I could graduate early. I was not about to walk the halls every day with people staring at me, pointing, and whispering behind my back any longer than I had to. I worked hard and in March of my senior year, I graduated. I left my friends, my cheer squad, gave up my senior prom, and the parties. I let the words of others get to me and decided I didn't deserve to walk down the aisle at graduation.

Instead, I watched from the stands as my friends celebrated their accomplishments. My boyfriend proudly wore his cap and gown and marched to his seat with his buddies. His face carried a huge smile, and there was no sign he had a baby on the way. I watched from the stands, eight months pregnant.

While my friends went off to college and lived out similar dreams I'd once had for myself, I spent time wondering how to buy a crib, diapers, and clothes. I was doing everything I could in preparation to have a baby, and get my life on track.

In June, I began taking college classes at the local community college and in July, with my boyfriend, mom, and friend by my side I gave birth to my daughter.

> "An unwanted pregnancy doesn't mean an unwanted child."

The waiting room was packed with expectant hearts ready to accept and love my precious baby girl. It was a day we celebrated and left the negativity of the past nine months behind.

Life as I knew it changed instantly! The first time I held her, I realized I made the right decision. All that hard work and sacrifice was worth it because now I had her. I looked down at this little person and broke down in tears. I was her mom. For the first time in my life, I saw myself in someone else's face.

Still, there was one problem. Everything she needed to survive was up to me and I hadn't the slightest clue how to do it. I had no idea how to take care of a baby.

I was still living at my mom and stepdad's house, which in and of itself was not great, because there was still so much tension about the pregnancy, the baby, the lies, and embarrassment. But I knew my mom was starting to come around. She always told me, "An unwanted pregnancy doesn't mean an unwanted child." She loved my daughter and allowed us to stay there, but I was basically on my own. She felt that since it was my decision to get pregnant, the baby was my full responsibility.

I lived with my mom while I fought to get back on my feet and plan my next move.

I returned to my college classes just four days after having my daughter. I was determined to get a college degree and provide for her. I tried to be the best mom I could, while also working a full-time job and struggling through exhaustion. My boyfriend's mom was a huge blessing and cared for my daughter when I needed her. My close friend had also gotten pregnant her senior year of high school and watched my daughter while she stayed home and cared for her twins.

Finally, I was able to get my own place when my daughter was four months old. We moved out and my friend and I got a small apartment together. I continued working a full-time job and attended community college full time.

My daughter's father moved away when she was three months old to go to college, so he was not a big part of her life. As a way to continue feeling normal, Saturday night was my night to party. I had to work very early on Sunday, so his mom would keep my daughter. I would party all night, drink alcohol and smoke pot and then go directly to work. It was my only outlet. This was not my dream life growing up! While my friends were at college, doing what we always talked about, I was changing diapers and being responsible for another human being.

Being a mother, I now understood where my mom was coming from. All the hopes and dreams she had for me, all came crashing down in a single moment. I had a lot of help from my friends and family as well as his parents, but at the end of the day, I was just a kid trying to raise a kid.

Things continued the same way for a few years—working full time, going to school off and on, moving from apartment to apartment, city to city, and relationship to relationship. I drove my daughter to Wenatchee once to visit her dad, and he didn't see her again until her second birthday. It seemed easy for him to continue living the life he wanted and I was left giving up my life to raise the daughter we both created. It wasn't easy, but I wouldn't change it for the world!

After spending six long months in Seattle trying to live out part of my dream of getting out of Yakima, I found myself fearful and desperate. My daughter got sick with a life-threatening illness. Luckily it was caught and cured, just in time.

I was completely broke, both financially and emotionally. While feeling lost, I added a few more broken relationships to my list. I became so extremely depressed that I was closer than ever to ending my life because I could no longer manage it. So I moved back to Yakima where I had the most help.

> at the end of the day, I was just a kid trying to raise a kid.

I went back to working full time and enrolled in massage therapy school. I met a guy who seemed to love me and loved my daughter. We dated for over two years. He proposed and we planned a Vegas wedding.

At the last minute, I felt something telling me to call it off. I ran from that relationship into the arms of a guy I met at work and started a relationship with him. I felt like I was in a good place and that he might possibly be the right one. This man was someone I knew I loved and cared about. I believed he loved my daughter and me; he had a great job, and took my daughter and me on incredible adventures.

However, things changed drastically when I once again found out I was pregnant.

My little girl was now five years old and was a smart, beautiful kindergartner. For the first time, I thought I had the family I always imagined I would have. We both had great jobs and discussed our future together, in depth. He informed me early in our relationship, that because of his religion and cultural background, he was forbidden to date me so I would never be able to meet his parents. I was okay with that since they lived in another country and felt honored he chose me in spite of what his parents would say.

He made it clear that *I am wanted.*

But when I told him I was pregnant, he responded with rage. Both of his hands grasped tightly around my neck and he began to choke me, while telling me I better have an abortion. I thought for sure my life would end that night. He stopped when he realized what he had done.

After not talking for several weeks, he began to embrace the situation with an open heart. However, I began being flooded with threatening phone calls from his family. His dad told me he would kill me if I kept the baby. I was offered a large sum of money to end the pregnancy, and was told that because he had gotten me pregnant and since I was not part of their religion, my baby would be a devil baby. I have never been so afraid in my entire life! I called the police to file a report but they could do nothing. The calls were coming from another country. I told them to make the report anyway so someone would know who killed me if I was murdered.

I pushed through my fear and knew I was supposed to keep this baby. Her dad decided to go against his family's wishes and stayed by my side.

I really hadn't given up my life, just chosen a different one.

As I drove to the hospital to welcome my second daughter into this world, my heart felt heavy. I wondered if I could love this baby as much as my first daughter. My oldest daughter and I went through so much. After all, we grew up together. However, as I held my newborn daughter in my arms that question no longer remained. For the first time ever, I found out that it's possible to love two people equally. As a mother, your heart doesn't have to choose and God makes enough room for both of them to be loved equally. The last six years had been the hardest years of my life, but all I had to do was look at her face and see that everything I gave up was worth it. Besides, I really hadn't given up my life, just chosen a different one.

He was an incredible dad, helpful financially as well as caring for all of us. The huge shift in him was incredible to watch and I felt extremely blessed. His job took him out of state shortly after our daughter was born but he came back to visit every weekend. Three months later, he bought a home and we moved in with him. It was our home and we were a family. I decorated the walls with family pictures, we picked out furniture together, and our future together looked like it would be a fairy tale ending.

Unfortunately, fast-forward eight months and my life went from a happy little family to uncertainty in the blink of an eye.

His cultural views of how a wife should act were something I would never be. I had been a single mom and was very independent. I hated how he tried to control me and tell me what to do.

The situation was getting worse every day so I called a friend and told her I needed to be out immediately. She and her husband showed up with a pickup and a trailer. We quickly packed my stuff while he was away at work. I found myself becoming a single mom, once again. This time I would have two girls to take care of; two little people who were depending on me.

I was jobless, I had moved three and a half hours away from home, and now I had nothing. I had been through this before so I knew I could overcome adversity again. I picked myself up and did what I had to do in order to take care of my girls. We moved back to my home city where I had the support of my parents, my oldest daughter's grandparents, her dad, and my friends. I was able to get us a little apartment and start over, again.

My second daughter's dad continued to be a huge part of her life. We became friends and stayed friends even when I was dating someone else. We were better as friends.

Then confusion hit us hard! We had a huge celebration for our daughter's third birthday. The day after the party, he went home to visit his family, and we never heard from him again. We found out that he met a woman who had the same religious and cultural beliefs as he did. This meant that in his world, the life he had with me never existed. He continued to send money each month to make sure our daughter was cared for—but all my daughter knew was that her daddy went to work and never came home.

Now my precious daughter had to walk through the same struggle I walked through, wondering if *she is wanted*. It broke my heart to see her hurt and abandoned.

I knew I couldn't let his choices stop me. I got a job and completed the training to become a nationalized pharmacy technician, and made a great life for the three of us. I was determined never to depend on anyone, to make my girls my first priority always, and never trust or give my heart away again.

I had a lot of healing to do, but as a single mom of two, working full time, and going to school again full time, I had to bury those hurts.

I not only had to learn the hard way once, but twice when it came to being a single mom. Even so, I wouldn't change a thing. I wouldn't trade a day I've gotten to spend with my girls for anything. They are my life and the reason I was put on this earth. I may never be famous. I may never make a big impact on others' lives. That's okay. I'm here to make a huge impact on the lives of my two precious daughters. They were always meant to be in my story. The broken relationships, the uncertainty of my own childhood and status as an adopted child, not knowing my biological parents and feeling unwanted, was all preparing me for this, for them. When they hurt, I can tell them I have been there and I hurt too.

I've experienced a lot of brokenness, disappointment, abuse, and betrayal in my lifetime. Some think I've experienced more than anyone should, and then again not nearly as much as others have. But I've also experienced a lifetime of love and support. I have met some amazing people and learned that some people are just not worth my time. I have learned that life is as hard as you make it, that everyone has a story, and that my story is no better than anyone else's.

If sharing my story can give one teen mom out there hope, guidance, and alleviate some fears, then being transparent has been worth it.

If any part of my story resonates with you, I want you to know it's not the end of your life—it's just the beginning! Just because you had a baby doesn't mean your hopes for college, a career, a home, or family can't happen. If anything, it should be the reason you try harder, the reason you don't give up, the reason you want to be more and do more.

Is it hard? Yes! A million times harder than I ever thought it could be.

Is it worth it? Absolutely! Being a mom has been more rewarding than anything else I have ever done in my life.

My girls are now sixteen and ten. I would not have learned the biggest life lessons without them. You don't always know what you think you know. One of the hardest life lessons to learn at eighteen was about friendship. Those I thought were my closest friends were the ones that pulled away when things got tough, when I was no longer the "popular cheerleader" but the pregnant outcast.

I spent so many years looking for love in all the wrong places, struggling with a broken heart, and it threw my life completely off track. Real love began to feel almost unreal. I once again began to believe the lie that I was unworthy of love.

Currently, I am happier than I've ever been—living in my own home, with my girls. I am happy with my career and the direction my future is headed. I recently graduated with my Bachelors of Science in health care administration with an emphasis in hospital management. My children are incredible and my oldest daughter told me that I'm her best friend. I feel incredibly blessed!

I realize now that if you're not happy with yourself, nobody else is ever going to make you happy. Loving and taking care of yourself is the most important thing you can do and will in turn allow you to love someone else.

Being a teen mom is not the end of your life.

Do I promote teen pregnancy? Absolutely not! That said, so much greatness could come from something which began in negativity. Life will be harder than you expected, but that is no excuse to give up. A positive pregnancy test is no reason to shut down and give up. It is an even bigger reason to strive for success. Your life is no longer just about you: It's about someone else, and that person is depending on you.

> My daughters may have not been in my plan, but they were in His.

I am slowly learning to love, and to be loved. To let down walls and begin trusting again. It'll take time and there's still a lot of healing to walk through. I have begun to rid my mind of lies and wrong thinking. I'm starting to understand and believe that through this entire journey I was loved. Not only by people, but also by a God I didn't even know. A God who was walking by my side my entire life. He is a God who can take even the worst situation and work it for good.

My daughters may have not been in my plan, but they were in His. Before I was ever formed in my birth mother's womb, God knew me! He knew my name, the day I was born, and He knows exactly where I came from and what my future holds.

I am forgiven for every mistake I made. He is unchanging, and I am perfect to Him. He is the perfect Father. He never left me, and above all I know...*I am wanted!*

Before I formed you in the womb I knew you, before you were born I set you apart; I appointed you as a prophet to the nations.
—Jeremiah 1:5 (NIV)

THE LOST GIRL

IT'S AMAZING HOW picture-perfect a family can look from the outside looking in. I felt like we had it all together, and to others it appeared as though we did.

In reality, that was far from the truth.

I was fifteen when my world fell apart. My dad's eyeglass business folded the same week that my mom kicked him out of the house. He moved to Seattle to look for work so we rarely saw him—we were stuck in Yakima with my mother. All my security was ripped out from under me, and I was a tiny piece of brokenness scattered on the floor.

> I found myself in a place where I no longer knew who I was.

We were left with no money, and my mom started drinking all the time. I was left to care for my brothers so she could try to work after all these years as a stay-at-home mom. It was extremely difficult for all of us! We went from looking like a rock-solid family to a giant mess. Family meant everything to me, and now it was gone.

I found myself in a place where I no longer knew who I was. I had no place to turn and suddenly realized that my entire life was a lie. I *felt completely lost.*

I began to hang out with people who were just as *lost* as I was. My friends and I did whatever we wanted, and our behavior was awful! There was no stable person in our lives watching out for us or trying to stop us. On several occasions, I would sneak out of my house at night knowing my mom would be too drunk to deal with me, so I never feared being caught. Everyone around me was drinking and smoking pot. Luckily, I was not able to participate very often because I got sick every time I tried. However, that didn't stop me from trying.

I hated school! I wanted to join the cheer or drill team so badly but didn't dare ask to try out because I knew my mom would just remind me how broke we were. I felt like I didn't really fit in with anyone. I always had to work hard to get good grades, but I had reached a place of not caring anymore. I no longer cared about my family, and didn't care what anyone thought about me. I was *lost!*

I met a boy during this season of my life who seemed to have it all together. He was sixteen, had a job and a car. I loved being around his family and was so desperate for security. I knew I couldn't remain on the path I was going down, and I found comfort in the things he and his family had to offer. I was so *lost,* I fell for anything, right or wrong, just to get another taste of the seemingly perfect life I thought I had before everything fell apart.

I started to believe that just maybe, together, we could create the family I had *lost.*

It didn't take long to realize how *lost* he was too. He was buried in his own insecurities and would do anything to keep me. I was desperate for love, security, and a family. We did nothing to prevent pregnancy and never thought twice about what we were doing. We both wanted to be grown up and live our own lives, but we had no idea what that actually looked like. We never stopped to consider how our actions would impact our family, or our own lives, forever.

When the pregnancy test came back positive, I was so excited! The woman at the pregnancy clinic tried desperately to get me to comprehend the seriousness of the situation. She didn't understand this was exactly what I wanted. In my fifteen-year-old mind, it made complete sense. I had no family at home, so this was going to be my family. I now had something growing inside of me that I would love, and it would love me back. I felt like I created something that would finally fill the emptiness, and now my life would be perfect once again.

I had no fear and truly believed this baby was the answer to all of my problems.

Although it seemed crazy to everyone else, it all made complete sense to me, and I didn't really care what anyone else thought. I knew my life would finally change, and that was all that mattered. A *lost* boy, joined by a *lost* girl, hoping to create a perfect family out of brokenness, expecting a baby to fill a void of love...this was how my story began.

I knew telling my mother about my pregnancy would be extremely difficult, and she would be angry. I also knew she would try to take control of the situation. Her life was a mess, so that was the last thing I wanted. My grandparents were very religious, so I knew that they, along with the rest of my family, would be embarrassed by my predicament. They all had opinions and were judgmental of my parents when they went through their separation, so I knew my situation wouldn't be handled any differently. I knew my grandparents loved me and wanted the best for me, but I believed I knew what I needed and wanted during that season of my life. My immaturity, and having no true grasp of reality, blocked all logical thinking.

At one point, my aunt tried to convince me to do an inter-family-adoption. The idea seemed ridiculous to me! I never considered abortion or adoption. I wanted a family. Now that I had created one, the thought of someone taking my baby from me was ridiculous! Because I had no idea what I'd gotten myself into, I had no fear and truly believed this baby was the answer to all of my problems. This was going to be great! We had no idea who we were, nor did we know much about each other. We had no plan of how we would support ourselves, let alone support a baby. Yet we were excited to be a family and never thought about the details that go along with it.

My family tried to hide my pregnancy as long as possible, but that became difficult as I quickly became bigger. I watched some of my friends enjoy school dances, join cheer and drill, and have opportunities I wanted to experience. My other group of friends continued down the dark path of partying and drugs, a path I'm sure I would have followed if I hadn't gotten pregnant.

At this point, I no longer fit in with either group of friends because of this choice to start a family. I wanted to finish school but knew this baby was coming way too soon, and there was no way to finish before she would be born. I attended an alternative school so I wouldn't feel like such an outcast. Other teen moms attended the school, and I thought this would be a way to enjoy this stage of my life. I took classes on parenting and cooking, as well as any other class I could take to try and learn how to be a wife and a mom.

I knew that neither of us were ready for what was coming. Reality was setting in quickly. What had we done?

My trips to the doctor's office were always difficult. I began to realize what I tried to create was not the same as the vision I had in my mind. I sat in the waiting room watching families pass by. They were full of joy—mature, married, able, and ready for a child. I was young, afraid, not ready, and unable to provide the life a baby deserves. However, the reality was that my baby girl was coming, regardless of whether I was ready or not.

I knew I had to be out on my own if I was going to survive, so my boyfriend and I decided being married was the answer to all our problems. In June, we convinced my father to drive us to Idaho, and just one month before I would become a mom, I became a wife. I cried the entire day, knowing deep down this wasn't the picture I had in my mind of where my life would be. We had a shotgun wedding, with no one around, a dress made to fit my pregnant belly, and I was marrying a man who seemed to be getting more and more *lost* by the minute. I still hadn't finished high school or even gotten my driver's license, and my baby girl would be here in only a month.

My husband was able to pull some money together because of a settlement he received from a horrible accident he was in as a child. We had just enough money for the down payment on his great grandmother's two-bedroom trailer house. His parents were able to get a loan for the rest and our house payment was only $175. Even that was a struggle to pay.

We did not live in a safe neighborhood. However, his grandmother lived across the street, his parents were just around the corner, and it was a roof over our heads. I took a break from school since my baby would arrive soon and I worked to pay the bills. I didn't realize you actually have to pay for water, power, phone, and everything else. This was definitely a wake-up call I wasn't prepared for. My husband lost the job he had when we met, jumped in and out of employment, and stopped going to school. We were constantly struggling with money, and barely made it from one paycheck to the next.

I chose to focus on where we needed to be, and I wasn't going to let anyone stop me!

The day our precious daughter was born was a mixture of pain, chaos, and clarity. When labor starts, it's truly not something you can change your mind about. Suddenly, you realize where the consequences of your choice put you and there's no turning back.

I wondered: *Would my husband be able to mature and help raise our daughter? Would I be able to? What if he doesn't? Can I do this on my own?* My daughter had no choice being born into chaos, and she was on her way. The room was packed with both of our families. Friends and extended family crowded the hallway. Everyone was excited to welcome this beautiful baby girl into the world. From the moment she was placed in my arms, I knew I would fight to make our life different. I would do whatever it took to get us out of this mess I created!

When we brought her home, I did my best to create something normal, even though I had no idea what "normal" looked like. My friends continued with life and enjoyed school. Meanwhile my relationship with my husband continued to spiral downward. I tried to set up a routine for my baby so she didn't feel the craziness that surrounded us. I had no one I could trust and no one to help. I knew that since I put myself in this situation, I had to make it my mission to change it.

I refused to see myself where I was: a teen mom, broke, no high school diploma, and no driver's license. I chose to focus on where we needed to be, and I wasn't going to let anyone stop me!

School started up again when my baby girl was just four weeks old, and although I struggled to leave her, I desperately wanted to finish my education. I also knew I had to find a way to make an income and support us. If I wanted to go back to school, I would need to work too.

I met with a counselor who helped me find a program at an alternative school that would allow me to attend school for half of the day and work the second half. I was lined up with a temp agency that set me up with a job at a Social Security office, which worked out perfectly because it was across the street from school. The daycare was also on campus, so I could remain close to my daughter the entire day. I knew this wouldn't be easy, but I was determined, and the counselor was a catalyst to encourage me and give me the confidence that I could do it.

She also set me up with a scholarship so I could start driver's education. I was so thankful for her help! My mom agreed to help out and give me a ride to driver's education the mornings my husband wouldn't wake up to take me, which ended up being almost every morning. We dropped my baby off at daycare, and then I was taken to my driver's education class. My grandparents would then pick me up from driver's education and give me a ride to school. After school, I would go to work and after work I would walk over to pick up my baby where either my husband would pick us up, or we would ride the bus home.

At home, I continued taking care of my baby with little help, finished my schoolwork, made sure the bills were paid, and worked up the determination to continue the same thing the next day. I hated dropping her off at daycare, but I had no choice. I was in complete survival mode!

This wasn't easy, but I knew this was the only way things would change, and I was willing to do whatever it took.

After finally finishing driver's education, my grandfather bought a car for me. It was the first gift I received from my family since I told them I was pregnant. They were adamant that since I wanted to live like an adult, I would have to do it with no help. Having a car was just enough taste of freedom to keep me going.

I continued going to school half a day and working. I loved not having to rely on others or the bus to get where I needed to go. While working at the Social Security office I took in everything that was around me. What did the successful people do to become more successful? How did they talk? What did they wear? I wanted to learn as much as I could to be able to make more money to support us. I took computer classes at school and any other class I thought would help me create a better future. Watching my mom struggle to find a job after being a stay-at-home mom with no work experience outside the home put a fear in me to learn as much as I could.

It was a lot of pressure for a sixteen-year-old—however, I had to remind myself that I was the one who'd put myself in this situation.

My job at the Social Security office was temporary and unfortunately ending soon. I had several part-time options on the table, but I knew they weren't enough.

I was eventually informed of a position opening at a bank where another employee's wife worked and was encouraged to apply there. I had three interviews, and they didn't seem very excited about hiring a young girl with a baby. I felt like I was under a police investigation during the interview process. I knew I had to prove to them that I could do the job and was mature enough to handle its demands.

There was one woman who was willing to give me a chance, and I got the job! The job wasn't full time and I didn't believe I could prove myself enough for them to keep me, so I worked another job in the customer service department at a grocery store. I worked at the bank during the day, and nights and weekends at the store. I was praying I could get enough money saved to move out of the hell we were living in, and praying they would keep me on at the bank.

Things continued to get worse between my husband and me. His moods would swing from one moment to the next. I had no idea if he was on drugs, or just crazy. I forced myself to focus on my daughter and remove my focus from him. The arguments became more frequent, and I knew he was never going to mature enough, or help in the way we needed him to, as a father or a husband. I was not willing to wait for him to get it together or sink us lower. I had to get my baby, and myself, away from him!

After a few months of working as hard as I could, the bank offered me a full-time position. I had great benefits, I made more money, and it was during the day so I could be home in the evenings. I finally had enough income and stability to leave my husband and the volatile situation he created at home, but I wasn't sure if I could make it on my own.

I decided to move in with my mom until I was confident I could do this by myself.

Although I felt defeated having to move back in with her, I knew it was better than where I was, and I would continue working hard to move us into a place of our own. I knew this next situation would need to be very temporary.

Once my daughter and I moved out, my husband walked away from the house we'd purchased and lost the money we used to buy it. I had no idea where he was living. He was not okay with the current situation, but was not willing to change. We were fighting like crazy, leaving me once again feeling defeated because I had sworn to myself and to her that she would never have to see this sort of mess. But sadly, I knew in my heart it was going to get even messier, and that he would be affecting our lives forever.

One evening I took my daughter out to visit his sister and to see her horse. He decided he wanted to come out and visit while we were there. As soon as he arrived, my stomach was in knots and I could sense something was wrong with him. He either was on something or extremely hung over.

He demanded to take our daughter. I refused, but offered to take her to his mom's house so he could see her. There was a flurry of threats, yelling, and cursing. I tried everything to get him to calm down, but nothing worked. Then he grabbed her car seat from my car, threw it in his, and ripped her out of my arms.

My heart dropped and I struggled to breathe! I jumped in my car with his sister and chased after him, ending at his mother's house. I ran to the car and grabbed my daughter out of the back seat. He quickly grabbed the car seat and threw it against the garage, then threw me against the car with our baby in my arms.

His mom witnessed the entire event and called the police. He quickly left once he knew the police were on their way. As I held my sweet, innocent baby in my arms, my mind was flooded with thoughts. What had I done? All I wanted was a family, and I created a nightmare! My sweet daughter deserved so much more, and I felt as though I had failed her.

Once we both calmed down, I placed the car seat and my daughter back in the car and drove away. I planned to find an attorney as soon as I could get to a phone.

At the age of seventeen, I was now filing for divorce. It took every penny I had saved to pay for an attorney, but I didn't care. I had to fight for my daughter!

The judge decided to allow supervised visitation, once a week, as soon as my ex-husband had a place to live and an income to provide for our daughter. The paperwork was sent out, giving him ninety days to respond. I spent the entire three months terrified of what he would try to do.

The time passed, and the day came for us to return to court. I had my mom by my side so I wouldn't be alone. My heart was racing when we entered the courtroom, unsure of what to expect. I felt extreme relief as I scanned the benches and realized that he had chosen not to show up. Within a few minutes, the judge looked over the paperwork and signed it. I had full custody of her, and he would be allowed weekly visits supervised by my mother since she was the only other person in the courtroom. He would also be required to pay $195 per month in child support to help with expenses.

With my divorce and custody finalized, I was able to put my focus back on finding our own place. I was excited not to be sleeping on my mother's couch anymore. I found a duplex I could afford, and saved the first six months' rent just in case. Once I moved, I left with no back-up plan. This had to work.

My ex-husband decided to move to Nashville, Tennessee, to pursue his dream of being in the music industry. I was grateful I no longer needed to worry about the chaos he would bring into our lives, yet saddened that my daughter would grow up without a dad, and sickened at how easy it was for him to pick up and walk away. I understood that sometimes your dreams have to change based on the decisions you made in life. It was now my desire to make her dreams come true. My baby girl was my responsibility, so if we were going to make it, it was up to me.

I went to work every day with a fire and a passion to learn as much as possible and advance as high as I could, to make a life for my baby girl and me. The downfall was that I was gone a lot more than I liked. I dropped her off early in the morning, seldom got off until after six in the evening, and most of the time she ate dinner at daycare before I could pick her up. We had everything we needed: food, clothes, and a place to live, but I was missing out on time with the most important thing in my life. Balancing time, and what I thought we needed in security of income, was something with which I struggled. My parents always struggled with income, and I was so terrified of repeating the same cycle.

I didn't want to date anyone, but hated being alone. I had a very rough time trusting any man, since I had been hurt so much. I feared the nights, having just her and me in the house. How would I protect us? I fought through many sleepless nights, shedding many tears. My roller coaster of thoughts left me feeling so *lost*!

I would talk to a God that I heard about in church when I was little and pray for protection, hoping He was real and would keep us safe. Putting my hope in God seemed like the only option, knowing I couldn't really do anything if someone broke in.

At this point, my daughter's dad had been gone for almost a year. He would send her gifts every now and then, but there was no other interaction. He would pay child support only when the government would take it from him. When he came back from Nashville, he would get to see her with supervised visitation, but would often be late, and she would sit there and wait. He was so angry that he had to see her under supervision, but I was so terrified of letting her go. He was so unpredictable! He taught my daughter that a daddy was simply a man who is never around, but sends lots of gifts.

I finally started hanging out with some childhood friends, as well as co-workers, and started to date occasionally, but could never get attached to anyone. Every person I met felt like a distraction to where I wanted my life to be. I had to be able to survive, without help from anyone. I had no real idea of what love was in a relationship. I only knew the love I had for my child, and that was what kept me alive and moving forward.

We both suffered feelings of abandonment, so I constructed emotional walls to protect us. If I don't let anyone get too close, there's no hurt when they leave, I thought. Who could really love me anyway? I was divorced, a teen mom, had a young child, and her dad constantly caused chaos in our lives.

I wanted to have the family I once dreamed of, but wasn't willing to risk more pain to get it.

Yet, at the same time, I had a strong desire to be around other adults. Of course, no one my age had children, so it was hard to do things that actually involved my daughter. Therefore, most of the time it was just the two of us. Occasionally, when I would go out and do something, it felt so wrong. I was a single mom and was constantly fighting the age I really was. I couldn't be twenty-one and enjoy the things other twenty-one-year-olds enjoyed, just as I wasn't able to enjoy being sixteen when I was sixteen. I hated carrying so much guilt all the time! I needed to be there for her, but I also really needed a break. I had to be both parents, and the sole provider.

Deep down inside, I continued longing for some sense of security and love—but had no idea what that looked like. I was completely *lost* in a jumble of emotions!

One night my friend got me to go out with her so I could be her designated driver. While we were out, I ran into one of my customers from the bank. He came in every Friday, but I never really talked to him. That night he decided to tell me he was very interested in me.

I did as I always did, and completely ignored what he said, and ran as fast as I could. Somehow, he got my phone number and decided to call me and apologize. We ended up talking for hours. We continued talking on the phone for a few weeks, and finally, I agreed to go out on a date with him.

This time seemed so different, but fear still clouded my mind. I was feeling a flood of emotions, which were so unfamiliar to me. With all my fears and insecurities of where this might lead, I still had to pursue it. He loved my daughter and wanted to get to know her, which was terrifying. What if he left? What if this wasn't the one…but what if he *was*? Would the walls I put up lead me to missing out on the life I dreamed of for us because I was afraid of getting hurt?

I always felt the world was looking at me, just waiting for me to fail. I couldn't show any weaknesses for fear someone might really see inside how scared I was. I believed that I had to prove to myself, and the world, that I could do everything on my own. It was amazing to see the things I could accomplish when I put it in my mind I had to. I was constantly trying to prove that I wasn't the label that many—but mostly *I*—had put on me.

I continued to hang on to my need to remain self-sufficient, and struggled with trusting he would stay. I had a lot of emotions and negative beliefs to work through during the time we dated. However, after a year, he proposed and I said yes without hesitation. This had to be different! I couldn't keep letting past mistakes, past failures, or the past failures of others, keep me from moving on with my life. I had to break the walls down, give us a chance as a family, and pray this was the right decision.

My daughter and I were both filled with joy and excitement about the wedding. We wore matching dresses, and had our hair done exactly the same. She was my maid of honor. I had saved up and had the wedding I always wanted. It was a perfect day! I felt like I was given a fresh start, and the family I prayed for. Nothing could ruin this incredible day—even when my dad showed up late, drunk, and had to be escorted away quickly before anyone could see him.

My dreams finally came true. I had a man who loved me and my daughter, and we loved him.

My daughter and her dad continued their off and on relationship. She wanted to see him, and I knew that having it supervised with my mom wasn't the best situation, but I was always terrified he wouldn't take care of her. He would live in town for a while and start to build a relationship, but then he would move again looking for something else. He was the fun "Disneyland" type of dad. He always wanted to buy her something or wanted to take her somewhere fun, but had no interest in actually being a parent or paying child support.

My husband and I had to play the not-so-fun parenting role. We made sure she did her homework and got good grades, provided medical insurance, met all her needs, and provided a stable home to live in, with rules. The problem with being the "fun" dad is when he ran out of money, she had no interest in being around him. He made many broken promises, and after a while, I watched sadly as my daughter built up her own walls for fear of being hurt.

One evening her dad called and was telling her that he was going to take me to court, and that because she was thirteen he would put her up on the stand to testify that my husband and I were bad parents. For the first time, I stepped back and let her answer for herself. I could no longer stand in the middle. I fought her battles up until that point, knowing I would be the bad guy in his eyes, and possibly hers. We wanted to raise her with strong standards, responsibilities, and give her a shot to live a life she truly deserved. We wanted her to be able to go to college, so grades were very important. We wanted her to be safe. Maybe I was a little too cautious when it came to her doing things, but I wanted her to have things I wasn't able to have, and that included a childhood. Now that she was a teenager, she had to start making decisions for herself.

My heart raced as I overheard her conversation with her dad. She told him, "Don't put me up there on the stand! I won't say I have bad parents, because they aren't, and I don't want to come live with you."

From that point on, their relationship crashed. He called her and wanted to take her on a summer trip. She didn't want to go, for many reasons, and he really didn't take it well. They ended up getting into a huge fight, and to this day have an estranged relationship. She simply says, "Once I realized I had outgrown my father in maturity, I no longer wanted to hang out with him."

This was a hard reality to face and very interesting to hear a teenager articulate that way. I am blown away by her maturity and strength!

My daughter was very interested in going to church, and when your teenager actually wants to go instead of hanging out with friends, it's quite an eye opener. We took her occasionally, but my heart wasn't in it. I was still haunted by bad experiences in church. I judged myself enough, and I really didn't need anyone else to judge me more.

Neither my husband nor I wanted religion in our lives. We both grew up in churches that focused more on rules than a relationship with Jesus, and we really didn't want to raise our kids that way. I never understood how you could act and look one way on Sunday morning and act completely different Monday through Saturday. When you confess your sins, but nothing ever changes in your life, what's the point?

Judgment from others was not what I considered love. I was so conflicted. Do I put my kids through that? I believed in God, but I never really understood the meaning of what that actually meant.

Even with all that running through my head, we went to church on occasion simply to appease my daughter. She was an impressionable teen, a big sister to a fiery red-headed sister eight years younger than her, and boy/girl twins thirteen years younger. We had to give church another try, and eventually found one that felt right.

As we grew in relationships with amazing people all around us, I had a very wise woman tell me, "Life is a choice for everyone. We all get to choose how we live. We don't have to live with our past mistakes, or the mistakes of those around us. Every day is a day you decide which way you go." I'm so grateful that just because I was raised in a mess, and my life started in a mess as a teen mom, I could still decide to finish it differently. Having positive people in my life has helped me realize the power I have in deciding what I want in my life and what I don't. There is so much power in a decision!

Looking back on what I walked through with my daughter, I carried so many moments of regret and guilt. I brought an innocent child into this world to try and fill the voids I had in my own life. I wanted a family and I wanted to feel loved. By the time I realized that a baby wasn't the answer, it was too late. But now I realize: Every day we get to use the strength we have gained from what we've learned and *decide* which way we want to go.

After I found out I was pregnant, I had one of two choices. I could live as a victim for the rest of my life, blame others, and remain stuck. Or I could decide to look in the mirror, take full responsibility for what I had done, and learn and grow in the process.

I chose to suck it up and grow. You too, have the power to decide.

I know there was a reason for my journey. I know my daughter would not be who she is today if her father was anyone other than who he is, and if we hadn't gone through what we did. She wouldn't be as strong, mature, or motivated as she is.

I know now that I was never alone. I have spent the last few years dealing with all my hurts and disappointments from the past. I have realized that God was with me the entire time. Every time I was afraid and praying, He heard me, held me, and comforted me. Even when I wasn't living the life I

There is so much power in a decision!

should have, God was the one who loved me unconditionally! When I was *lost, He guided me.*

My relationship with Jesus has helped me grow, forgive, and love deeper than ever before. My love for my husband is stronger, and I'm a better mother. The security I was always longing for was in Jesus. He was the void in my heart that nothing else could fill.

God is a perfect Father and the perfect family I was in search of was in Him. He took care of me and protected me. He heard my every prayer. He is a perfect friend and loves me no matter what. I found myself in Him—and when I realized that, I finally saw the truth, and I was no longer *the lost girl.*

Then Jesus told them this parable: "Suppose one of you has a hundred sheep and loses one of them. Doesn't he leave the ninety-nine in the open country and go after the lost sheep until he finds it? And when he finds it, he joyfully puts it on his shoulders and goes home. Then he calls his friends and neighbors together and says, 'Rejoice with me; I have found my lost sheep.'"

—Luke 15:4-6 (NIV)

THE COMPROMISE

I OFTEN WOKE up to the aftermath. A broken glass door seemed to pique my curiosity, instead of deep concern.

From the time I could remember, my parents fought. Usually it was because my dad drank too much. Sometimes I would just lie in bed and listen to them, and other times I would wake up to the destruction. I was never told what actually happened, so I learned to be satisfied with whatever lie they came up with, such as: "Dad locked himself out, so he had to break the glass to get in."

The truth was he got way too drunk and became destructive. My parents wouldn't talk, and issues were simply swept under the rug.

My brother and I spent a lot of time at home alone. Both of my parents worked full time, so after-school and summer breaks were spent unsupervised doing whatever we wanted. My brother would lead us to do crazy things that could have gotten us injured or killed. During my elementary school years, he brought home inappropriate videos that he forced me to watch, and made sure I knew the meaning of every new slang word he learned from his friends at school. He sexually molested me for many years and filled my head with disgusting lies.

Eventually, my brother started getting into drugs and because he was my babysitter, I went along with him to pick up weed. He did not protect me as an older brother should and created deep wounds that seemed impossible from which to heal. I told no one what was happening inside our home and didn't talk to friends about the shame I carried. My fear of my brother kept me silent and cooperative.

By the time I reached middle school, my half-brother was arrested for drug use and a few other charges, and spent some time in prison. He wasn't someone I could look up to or turn to for protection either.

During these early years of my life, I learned to deal with problems by sweeping them under the rug and pretending everything was fine. I allowed shame to silence me, and hid everything with a smile painted on my face.

This painful beginning led to years of struggling…

When a police officer became my soccer coach in eighth grade, I decided I would pursue a career as a police officer so I could arrest guys like my brothers. I felt like if I were ever going to be protected, carrying a badge and a gun was my only hope; however, until then I would have to continue my secret struggle.

We may have looked great in family photos, but so much was taking place in our home. My parents' marriage was rapidly deteriorating, and eventually they divorced.

My mom went through a season of being almost unrecognizable. She cut her hair very short, double-pierced her ears, pierced her belly button, and bought a sports car. She quickly entered into a relationship with a guy from work and remarried.

It was in this season of not knowing which way was up that my life was saved by a horse. I was caught in a whirlwind of chaos and confusion, and I think God knew exactly what I needed during this mess. There seemed to be a horse-sized hole in my heart, and nothing else could fill it. My horse trusted me and accepted me with all of my hurt and all of my shame. He was strong, solid, and carried me when the burden was so heavy, I couldn't carry myself. This may seem like an unimportant detail, but without that horse I'm not sure where I'd be.

As I entered into high school, I watched my friends sift through boyfriends, suffer breakups, and be so in love nothing else mattered. I wanted nothing to do with that! High school years were supposed to be fun, and adding in a boyfriend seemed like the last thing I ever wanted to do. Having unhealthy relationships with my two older brothers helped me keep my mind off of boys, at least for a little while...

I had always been just "one of the guys," and had several guy friends. However, over time our games of capture the flag turned into a day of flirting with one of the guys in the group. My heart would flutter when we spent time together and his feelings started to shift as well. Towards the end of our sophomore year of high school, we were officially "together." I still got to be "just one of the guys" and we were content just hanging out; however, over time, our feelings continued to grow. We talked about being together forever and I truly believed we were in love.

After being together for almost a year, I could tell that he had started to get crap from his friends who'd already had sex, many with several girls. I remained one of the few of my friends to still be a virgin. I wanted to wait for the man I planned to marry, out of fear of getting a bad reputation. I finally reasoned with myself that since we loved each other and I was sure we would be married, it would be okay.

I wanted to take the time to make really sure we were being safe. A friend of mine received a prescription for birth control by telling her mom she was having severe menstrual cramps. I decided to try that route too, and it worked! I talked to my boyfriend about my concerns and my feelings about abortion. I told him that if we decided to have sex and if I were to get pregnant, abortion would not be an option. He told me not to worry and we would cross that bridge if we ever came to it. He reassured me that sex was really not that big of a deal since we loved each other. I began to let my guard down. I trusted him, and started to align my beliefs with his.

That was where *The Compromise* began.

The heart necklace he bought me on Valentine's Day was beautiful! I decided that night I would finally *compromise* my beliefs. His parents weren't home, so we had the house to ourselves. I trembled with fear, but couldn't figure out why. The gift he bought me wasn't cheap, so I couldn't change my mind now. Wasn't this supposed to be exciting, the night every girl waits and longs for? Something about this felt wrong, but it had to be right since most of my friends had been having sex since freshman year and had great stories to share.

That night I gave into peer pressure, *compromised* everything I believed, and because of that night, our relationship changed forever. I left his house with tears running down my face and feeling dirty. Why did I feel this way? I thought this would bring us closer. This was not how my friends told me it would be!

Our relationship was never the same again. I lost all dignity and put up with anything and everything he did. He seemed to walk with his head a little higher, and mine sunk a little lower. I strived to be the best girlfriend possible so he wouldn't break up with me, but the more I tried, the worse he began to treat me.

By the end of my eleventh grade year, friends started to notice the change.

My boyfriend had me so wrapped around his finger that he could do anything and say anything and I would just take it. I felt absolutely broken down from the constant emotional abuse. He punched holes in the wall when he was angry. I promised myself I would leave if he ever hit me—yet when that time came, it still didn't put an end to the cycle. He would remind me how much smarter than me he was and cut me down in front of his friends.

I was no longer pretty enough, so he would break up with me, and in the same week ask me to be his girlfriend again.

I became so wrapped up in trying to please him that I was no longer myself and my friends begged me to break up with him. Some of his friends would even ask me why I put up with what I did. The only reason I could come up with was because I loved him. He was so much different when we were alone, so I hung onto that. I stayed because he told me he loved me and I held onto those words, even when his actions didn't line up with them. I remained hopeful things would change back to the way they were before *The Compromise.*

At home things remained chaotic. I bounced back and forth between each parent's house. When I didn't like how things were going at one parent's house I would go stay with the other parent. There was no set visitation and I thought my mom was nuts when she tried to create one.

When my mom's relationship with her new husband didn't work out, they divorced. My mom decided to move to the Seattle area for a new start, and since I was going into my senior year of high school, I refused to go with her.

My dad married a woman I didn't get along with, so I moved in with a good friend. I had two families who offered to take me in. I was loved by both; however, one had strict boundaries in place and would require I attend church, and the other one offered freedom. I was desperate for some stability in my life, but not at the expense of being able to live life the way I wanted.

Although my relationship with my boyfriend was not the best, I made him and his family my everything. His parents also moved to the Seattle area so he moved in with his sister. They allowed me to stay the night whenever I wanted. We both lived without rules or boundaries, and we took full advantage of it. They became my family while mine continued falling apart, and I grew very close to them.

The great thing about birth control is you know exactly when your period is supposed to come. After taking the white pill for three days and nothing happening, I knew something had to be wrong! I called one of my best friends and she agreed to go to the store for me. I drove over to her house with my heart racing. I didn't remember missing a pill so surely the test would be negative. She purchased a two-pack, just to make sure we got an accurate response. I went to the bathroom with the box in hand, pulled out the instructions, and began to read.

I took a deep breath, and pulled the cap off the first test. The test said to wait several minutes for the results—however within seconds I was staring at two pink lines. This test had to be wrong since two lines meant pregnant! I tried not to freak out as I slowly pulled out the second test. When that test showed the same results, I felt like I was going to puke! My eyes filled with tears and I knew I had to get to my boyfriend's house to tell him.

I entered with the key his sister gave me since it was pretty late and most everyone would have already fallen asleep. I unlocked the door and quietly walked

> I was desperate for some stability in my life, but not at the expense of being able to live life the way I wanted.

through the living room and entered his room. I crawled in bed next to him and started to sob.

"What's wrong?" he asked several times.

I couldn't bring myself to tell him, but I knew I had to. "I'm pregnant," I cried.

I looked up at him with puffy eyes, waiting for him to tell me everything would be okay. Half smiling, he replied, "Well, we can't keep it."

His reaction took my breath away. Maybe I misread his smirk or misunderstood what he had just said. The tears began to flow again.

He kept holding me in his arms, but it wasn't comforting. I felt like throwing up. Did he really just say that? I had been very clear with him that I would never have an abortion. Now we were crossing that bridge he didn't want to talk about, and now it was too late. Sweeping things under the rug wasn't going to work and neither would pretending.

At that point in my life, I was on track for graduation and was volunteering as a Police Explorer to pursue my dream of becoming a police officer. I had a job working at the front desk of the detectives' division at the police department. I was on the cheer squad at school, ran track, was part of school leadership, on the honor roll, and I had plans to join the military as part of the Military Police program when I graduated. I wanted to be a success story in my family. I had my goals in line and the determination to pursue them. What would I do now? Where would I live? I couldn't expect the friends I was staying with to open their home to a baby too. I felt so lost! How could one *compromise* lead to such a mess?

When I began to tell people, it seemed like everyone had the perfect answer. "You will ruin your life if you don't end that pregnancy. Get an abortion! It will hurt a lot less than childbirth."

My school counselor had children he had adopted and encouraged me to consider that option. My boyfriend promised we would stay together if I had an abortion. The rumors started spreading like wildfire. News got to friends before I could tell them, and my coach asked me to leave the cheer squad. Random people called the school to see if I was interested in adoption.

I remember one voice that gave me hope. With tears in my eyes, I went to a man whom I'd looked up to since he was my soccer coach in middle school. He gave me a big hug and said, "Congratulations." My heart dropped! No one had said that to me and it felt good. For the first time, I didn't feel judged and the realization that I was going to be a mom started to take hold.

It took some extra time for me to work up the nerve to tell my dad. I wasn't afraid of him. He was the hardest to tell simply because I worked so hard to not disappoint him. I felt like I was his last hope of raising a kid that didn't "mess up," and now, I had let him down. I couldn't get the words to come out of my mouth before my eyes were full of tears. I think I got out just enough syllables for him to figure out what I was trying to say. He gave me a huge hug and made me feel like everything would be okay.

My first trip to the doctor was difficult. I remember sitting in the waiting room filling out the paperwork, feeling like I had people staring at me from all directions.

I was nervous as I lay on the table waiting for the ultrasound technician to enter the room. It still hadn't set in that I was pregnant. The ultrasound gel felt warm and the monitors everywhere were enough to keep me distracted. The silence felt uncomfortable, and the words that came next took my breath away:

"It's twins."

My heart dropped! I couldn't believe it! What now? My boyfriend didn't want anything to do with one baby—what would he say about *two?* I felt sick to my stomach, and the room seemed to be spinning. I honestly don't remember what happened during the rest of that appointment. I was in complete shock!

My pregnancy was a roller coaster ride. After the first three months, once my boyfriend realized I wasn't going to change my mind about having an abortion and I was already too far along anyway, he left me.

However, after I begged and pleaded with him, he agreed to come to my twenty-week ultrasound. I was hopeful that once he saw them and heard the babies' heartbeats, he might feel differently. He also agreed he would go with me to purchase the first outfits once we found out if they were boys or girls.

> My focus became graduating, surviving, and preparing to be a mommy.

As I lay on the table, I would shift my eyes between the monitor and his face, hoping for some kind of positive reaction. He remained emotionless. When the nurse announced that she saw two girls, his face became stone cold. A day I had hoped would change things and be joyful, turned out to be everything but that. I was excited to be having two girls, but seeing his disappointment brought on a cloud of sadness.

As we left the doctor's office, he demanded that I take him home. When I tried to talk to him, anger filled his eyes and his fist slammed into my window with rage. He told me if I didn't start driving he would start walking and never talk to me again. Tears poured from my eyes and we remained silent the rest of the way back to his house.

I continued going to school and took extra classes so I would be able to complete my graduation requirements early. My friends had schedules loaded with fun elective classes and enjoyed their senior year. I felt sick all the time, continued to get bigger, and looked more and more pregnant every day. I learned to ignore the constant whispering and staring.

I could no longer be involved in any cheer squad activities or any other school events and felt completely alone. Our cheer squad went to the extreme of retaking the team photo without me or my friend who was also pregnant. I no longer had a vision for my life and took each day as it was thrown at me. My focus became graduating, surviving, and preparing to be a mommy. My entire future was turned upside down, all because of one *compromise*!

My ex-boyfriend continued on with his life without me. He dated girls that knew about my pregnancy, but that didn't stop them. We became strangers and he would barely make eye contact with me. I felt judged by him as though he had nothing to do with the situation. Sitting at a desk at school started to get more and more uncomfortable, and my frequent trips out of class to use the bathroom or throw up were frowned upon by teachers. Missing class when I was too sick to attend school was not given any special consideration: "If you miss it, you fail." My grades went down, but I continued to fight and earned enough credits to graduate.

While my friends enjoyed their last few months of school, I was placed on bed rest and not allowed off the couch unless I was going to the bathroom or a doctor's appointment. I was so uncomfortable and thought my skin would rip any day. I ended up in the hospital for several days at twenty-eight weeks along to stop labor, and a few more times after that. I was sent home with prescription drugs to stop contractions and did my best to keep the babies in as long as I could.

Graduation came with many mixed emotions. I was so excited to have made it, but looked huge in my graduation gown. Many students didn't think I should be allowed to walk because it would "look bad," yet there was no debate about whether my ex-boyfriend should walk or not. Or what about all the girls that had decided to have an abortion? Hadn't they made the same *compromises* for which I was now being judged?

Through all the craziness, my best friend stuck by my side and we walked it out together. I felt eyes staring at me from the stands and my family listened to comments from every direction. But I pretended none of that mattered. I had fought hard to finish school and I was getting my diploma.

Then four days later, at thirty-six weeks, my water broke!

I was home alone and had no idea what to do. I wasn't in pain, but knew I needed to get to the hospital. I called my friend to give me a ride, and informed my ex-boyfriend that today was the day, just in case he wanted to be there. I was hoping by some chance, once he saw his baby girls, he would change his mind. I was disappointed when he didn't come, but knew I had to change my focus.

My family and a few friends were by my side. This was the day my world would change forever, and I would become a mom.

The operating room was cold and I was frightened. My doctor hadn't explained to me that I wouldn't deliver in a normal room. I was moved to an operating room to deliver my babies. Birthing twins was considered to be a high-risk delivery since the chances of something going wrong were increased.

The room was filled with several nurses, two incubators, and a couple of NICU (Neonatal Intensive Care Unit) doctors. I started to wonder if something was wrong but didn't ask for fear that someone would judge me for asking a stupid question. Everyone was silent and seemed to have concern written all over their faces. My mom was by my side and helped keep me calm.

Eight hours after my water broke, my beautiful baby girls arrived just three minutes apart.

Just one look into their eyes, and the world seemed to stand still. Never had I known a love like this before. As I held my baby girls together in my arms for the first time, all the heartache I experienced during my pregnancy suddenly disappeared. I was their mommy! I knew this journey would not be easy, but I also knew that my determination would make it possible.

My ex-boyfriend showed up to the hospital with five of his friends, the night before we were supposed to go home. They all filtered through the room to see the girls, then left. My mom told him he could stay as long as he wanted, but he stayed for less than an hour. As he held the girls in his arms, I felt sick to my stomach. The look on his face was so hard to read and honestly, I had a hard time even looking at him. I wasn't sure how I should feel...angry and bitter because he hadn't been around, or hopeful that he might want to be a daddy. I didn't know what to say, so I remained silent. My heart and mind were racing so I couldn't just close my eyes and rest either. I had no idea what the future was going to look like. All that mattered from that day forward were my two precious babies, whether he stuck around or not.

> I knew this journey would not be easy, but I also knew that my determination would make it possible.

For the first couple of months, I lived between my dad's house in Yakima and my mom's in Seattle. It was hard when my mom would come to visit at my dad's because of the awkwardness between my mom and stepmom. So I packed up both babies when they were only a few days old to stay with my mom, then returned every other week to my dad's so I could attend a parenting group full of other moms of twins. My stepmom also became a big help and we finally developed a relationship. I was desperate for help with the babies so I went where I could get it most.

The girls' father would stop by very occasionally with a car full of friends and stay for a very short amount of time, until it was time for him and his friends to go out. He never stayed long enough for them to wake up or help with anything, which frustrated my dad. He was offended when my dad asked that he come alone if he wanted to visit. The visits stopped after that. I continued to try to keep him involved and even offered to take the babies to his house. I would make plans with him to visit his grandparents' house, but then he wouldn't answer when I would call. I had to make visits fit into his schedule or he wouldn't see the girls. Then he would get angry with me and blame me for how little his family saw them. He never wanted to help, but had no problem making demands. This cycle got exhausting and I eventually stopped trying.

The local Mothers of Multiples group continued to be a resource for which I was incredibly grateful. It was a huge support when I was pregnant, but now became a lifeline after having the girls. I was surrounded by other moms with twins, or triplets, who treated me like any other parent of multiples. They helped me be a better mom, and problem solve how to raise twins. They brought meals when the girls were first born, passed down clothes, and gave me resources. This became a safe place, one in which I was not judged. I was just a woman trying to be a good mom like everyone else in the group.

I once again discovered how much I craved stability and traveling was becoming exhausting. I moved the three of us into our very own apartment when the girls were just a few months old. I watched a friend's baby during the day so I could be home with the girls, then I worked at an after-school program in the afternoon and a tanning salon at night. I fought to make ends meet, but things seemed to always work out.

I loved that I was able to be home with the girls during the day, but fought through exhaustion having to work two jobs in the evening. I wasn't afraid of hard work, and accepted that this is what my life was going to look like. I knew my plan to go into the military or become a police officer anytime soon was no longer an option, and I was okay with that. I was willing to do anything for my daughters, so placing a dream on hold felt easy.

I received help from the state in the form of food stamps, medical assistance, and some cash. I hated the looks I would get when I had to hold up the grocery store line using my WIC coupons, but I didn't really have another choice. I would grocery shop late at night and choose lines that no one else was in to use my food stamp card, hoping no one would notice.

My first year as a young mom with twins was going pretty well. I was able to spend a lot of time with my babies. The girls were always dressed well. They never went without, we had a nice apartment, and I was the best mom I knew how to be. I also had help from family, was able to pay my bills, and honestly, I felt relatively comfortable.

The girls were almost a year old when I got up the nerve to write their father an e-mail. He had moved over three hours away and did not leave me a phone number or address. I had to ask his friends to get his new e-mail address.

I was shocked when he responded and agreed to see the girls. His letter explained that going away to college was best for him and the girls in the long run, and that he wouldn't be able to make it back to visit until summer break.

Although it felt like a flood of excuses and garbage, I knew I had to fight for my girls to have a daddy in their lives. So I kept my thoughts to myself. That very next week I loaded up the girls and took a trip to Seattle for him and his parents to see the girls. We spent three full days with them. I dressed the twins in their cutest outfits and was once again hopeful that he just might want to stick around this time.

He decided to move back to Yakima over the summer. He told me he wanted to be closer so he could be around to help more with the girls.

However, after being back for only a few weeks the excuses started again.

One situation with my girls' father honestly changed the course of my life forever, and I am truly grateful for it.

He had agreed to watch the girls one day while I went to work. He drove up just as I had finished loading the car seats and babies into my car. He was late and I told him I had made other arrangements because I couldn't chance losing my job. He shouted out a few cuss words, and then proceeded to tell me I was worthless and would never make anything of myself, then sped off. Those words, although hurtful, lit a fire in me that ignited a hunger for change. I didn't know yet what that change would look like, but this event opened my eyes

just being "comfortable" wasn't enough anymore.

to the reality that I needed to do something different. That just being "comfortable" wasn't enough anymore. I suddenly had a hunger to prove my worth and to prove I could make something of myself.

The summer was ending and I continued to try to make things work so the girls would have a dad. I talked to my mom about staying with her so that I could attend the community college close to her in Everett. That would also allow the girls' father to be closer to the girls, and I would have help from my mom to care for them while pursuing my degree.

We planned a trip to the Seattle area to visit some of the colleges. While on our way, my car broke down on the side of the freeway. He called his mom to pick us up and became extremely angry. Since there wasn't enough room in her truck, he suggested we just travel down the freeway with the babies on our laps. I refused to put them in danger traveling anywhere without car seats, so he jumped in the truck and abandoned us on the side of the road.

Things continued to spiral downward. He was gone once again with no attempt to contact us.

I knew that regardless of what his plans were at this point, I had to pursue change. I didn't want to live in an apartment or stay on state assistance for the rest of my life. I had to do something different for my precious babies. I also had to realize and be okay with the fact that I would be continuing this journey on my own, without any help from him.

I knew if I stayed "comfortable," I would live with regrets. I knew I had to go back to school and pursue a college degree. I decided to go ahead with my plans to stay with my mom and register for classes at Everett Community College. I was blessed with two beautiful babies who deserved a better future. I decided from that day forward not to let his hurtful words hold me back or distract me. Instead, I chose to look at it as a friction that made me uncomfortable enough to push out of my comfort zone.

His words became my catalyst for change!

I had never planned to go to college. I hadn't seen it as an option in my future. Not only did I believe the lie that I wasn't smart enough, but no one in my immediate family had made it that far. I realized, however, that was my family's history, not my future. I was determined to do something different and to be something different.

I walked into Everett Community College completely blind. I knew nothing about which classes to take, the different degrees, graduation requirements, or credits. I just knew the first step was to figure out how to sign up for as many classes as I could to be in college for the shortest time possible.

My college days were an absolute blur! I was taking twenty-five to thirty credits at a time, working at the daycare on campus where the girls stayed when I was in class, and staying up late to finish my work. My social life consisted of schoolbooks and babies. I would try to sneak off to the gym every once in awhile, but most of my free time was consumed with playing at the park, and trying to pass my classes.

On days I struggled, my baby girls fueled me, and the hurtful words once said to me continued to push me to work harder.

I started dating off and on, but the guys I chose were not good influences. I felt unworthy of being loved by a quality man because I'd messed up so badly. I told myself that no man would want a young mom with two kids, so I hung around any guy who asked me out, or told me I was pretty.

I continued to tell myself that since I'd already had sex, it really wasn't a big deal. I would pour myself into relationships and get little in return. Each time I would try to heal my heart, give it away, and have it returned torn apart.

that was my family's history, not my future.

My walls finally came up when one of the guys I was dating asked me why I continued letting him treat me the way that he was. I had no answer to his questions, but never saw him again. This was another wake-up call, which created a hunger in me for change. I had to keep my focus on school and my babies. I could no longer depend on a man to show me my worth!

Eventually, I moved into my own apartment with my adorable, almost two-year-old roommates, so I could be closer to school. I completed my two-year degree in a year and a half, and enrolled at a CWU (Central Washington University) campus near Seattle, seeking my degree in Psychology and Criminal Justice in hopes of pursuing a career as a police officer.

However, when I learned how long I would need to be away from my girls to attend the police academy, I started to look deeper into why I really wanted to be a police officer. I loved working with broken people and rescuing kids from abusive homes. I truly loved being on the "rescuing" side of law enforcement, which led me to pursue a school counseling degree.

During this time, I also met my current husband. We had decided we wanted to pursue a relationship, but he lived in Portland and Seattle was more than a three-hour drive away.

The long distance relationship was difficult! After several trips back and forth and many long phone calls, we felt like we were meant to be together.

We married after dating only five months. We had opinions flying at us from every direction. We had a small and simple wedding in a friend's backyard surrounded by many people who thought we were doing the wrong thing.

I wasn't sure myself if we were doing the right thing, but had it stuck in my mind that it was what was best for my daughters. After the wedding, the girls and I moved to Portland, away from my friends and everything I knew. Even though I was newly married, I felt alone.

Finishing school was a battle. I began commuting two and a half hours twice a week back to the CWU campus near Seattle to finish my degree. Then with only one quarter to go, I was told the rest of the classes I needed for my degree were only offered at the main college campus in Ellensburg.

There was no way I was willing to slow down or stop now. So for the spring semester, the girls and I moved back in with my dad in Yakima and I made the daily forty-five-minute commute to school every day. I was taking twenty-five credits, and drove back to Portland almost every weekend to spend time with my husband. Through babies getting sick on finals day, exhaustion, tons of miles on my car, and a couple speeding tickets, I graduated with my Bachelors degree with a major in Psychology.

I was grateful for my husband's patience during this time. However, marriage wasn't all I thought it would be. After dating such a short time, I quickly realized how little we knew about each other. We were two broken people, carrying stuff from our past, which we had never dealt with or healed.

Neither of us were raised in homes with good marriages, leaving us to bring only what we knew, and try to make it work. I noticed the same cycles of unhealthy communication and pretending that I saw in my parents' marriage starting to show up in my marriage. I continued to be really good at pretending and sweeping every struggle we had under the rug.

It felt like we were two puzzle pieces being forced together and never able to fit correctly. I wanted to run, but felt like if I walked away from my marriage, I would fail once again. Our first year together was very rocky, and instead of building trust, I built walls. Something had to change!

Although I was never raised in a church, I decided it would be good for the girls to be in a place where they were surrounded with good people. I went only for them, and planned to simply go through the motions of sitting through church on Sundays. Yet slowly I started to feel my heart soften. We met some amazing people who had been in the same place we were and shared their testimony of healing. We were baptized together and grew in our faith. I started to feel hope that we could make our marriage work.

We welcomed a handsome son into our family two months before I graduated with my M.Ed in School Counseling degree. The day I graduated I felt like I had conquered the world.

Less than a year later I was hired on as a freshman counselor at a high school in Vancouver, Washington. A year after that we completed our family with another precious baby boy. I was proud of my accomplishments and felt extremely blessed to be the mother of four incredible children.

We looked amazing in our family photos, but things continued to fall apart. After we moved, we stopped going to church. We both had solid careers, but our lives were falling apart. We rarely spoke unless we were arguing and didn't enjoy time together. Our children experienced horrible fights and were often exposed to us yelling. They watched us as we floundered around trying to have a healthy marriage but never taking steps toward making it happen.

The more my marriage fell apart, the more I buried myself in my counseling career, trying to make the lives of my students improve. I was good at what I did, but came home every night to my mess. I tried to play super mom at home, but I was exhausted. I felt like a single mom, and tried my best to hold everything together. My husband found his identity in his career as a firefighter, and eventually found friendship and romance with another woman who built him up emotionally and paid attention to him. This led to bigger wounds, taller walls, deeper hurt, more anger, and no trust. We swept it under the rug because that was easy and familiar.

From the outside looking in, no one would have known we were struggling. We attempted to buy happiness, yet with each purchase we continued to feel empty and added more financial stress that tore our marriage further apart. We were digging ourselves into a hole that seemed impossible to get out of.

Again, I realized something had to change, but change takes work! I knew if I wanted to end this cycle I had to do something completely different and stop pretending...

After several years of counseling, prayer, support groups, and a couple of separations, I hired an attorney and filed for divorce. I believed deep down that I had tried everything to make my marriage work. For too many years we tore each other apart, blamed each other, learned to pretend, and built solid walls that couldn't be broken. I thought it was the only way for the cycle to end and not get passed down to my children.

That is when God stepped in and changed everything.

After thirteen years of an unhealthy marriage, the end became our beginning. It took all of this for both of us to finally realize that you no earthly thing or person can fill that God-sized hole you have in your heart, except God Himself.

can't have a healthy marriage when you both have walls up. God couldn't work in our marriage until we got to the end of ourselves. We had to allow our marriage to be buried before we could grow something new, the way God intended it. He had to wake us up, to begin to fight for our marriage instead of against it.

God is teaching us to look to Him instead of each other, to face the traumas from our past and grow from them. We are learning the power of two whole people coming together to create a family, and seeking the company of people that live the life we want for our family. A child doesn't just need any family; he needs a healthy one. I am excited for this new journey of allowing our mess to become our message.

Although I felt alone many times in my life, I have a clearer view looking back now. I spent so many years living for the world, seeking love in all the wrong places. What I now know, years later, is that no earthly thing or person can fill that God-sized hole you have in your heart, except God Himself. I was never alone! He was there by my side, loving me, guiding me, protecting my baby girls, and protecting me.

Even before I knew Jesus, He was there! He loved me through every *compromise*, every mistake and every hard time. He saw and continues to see the real me, and I don't have to fake a smile, sweep things under the rug, or hang pretty pictures up to pretend everything is okay. He is the perfect Man, who is a perfect Husband, perfect Father, and perfect Friend. Through Him, I have learned what it means to dream without limitation. I no longer carry shame or feel unworthy. He is my Healer and my Comforter, and He is that for my children and husband too. And although I still have a burning passion and love for horses, I now allow Jesus to be the strength that carries me when I am not strong enough.

I know how it feels when that pregnancy test comes back positive. Your world feels like it has been turned upside down. You may feel like the hopes and dreams for your future are over. However, you have the power to decide whether your past defines you, or *refines* you! To be an overcomer or allow yourself to be buried in self-doubt, shame, and allow your past to hold you back.

This road will not be easy, but it's so worth it. Allow this to be your *starting point* and step out of your comfort zone. Pursue the dreams you carry in your heart. If you don't, you'll live with regret. You may be young, you may be afraid, but being a teen mom doesn't have to slow you down. To the contrary, let it ignite a fire within your heart to do more and be more than you ever thought possible.

I encourage you to surround yourself with people who will speak life over you, who will believe in you when you don't believe in yourself, guide you as a mom, and encourage you to be transformed.

Don't get caught off guard! Decide who you want to be, set your goals, be solid in your beliefs, and stick to them. *Compromise* is sneaky. It happens one day at a time, until it knocks you completely off your feet. Your entire life can be turned upside down because of one decision, good or bad. *Compromise* finds you in your weakest places and can leave you feeling like a failure, wishing you could turn back time.

The *compromise* I made left me feeling broken and hopeless. I had to face things I never wanted to face and take my girls on a journey that had a lot of rough roads. I had dreams that had to shift, and I had to grow up fast. However, I am forever grateful for the journey and the two blessings that came out of it.

The adversity I faced in my past made it difficult for me to trust, and I had to learn to forgive. My girls had to face feelings of abandonment and not being "good enough" because of their biological dad's decision to walk away. However, through it all we have gotten stronger and have a story to share. For so long adversity silenced me. Yet sharing my story has helped me find my voice. Our roller-coaster ride is now our testimony. Though you may have started weak or you might find yourself feeling like a failure, you can still finish strong. You can turn your mess into a message of hope and encourage others when they find themselves a little off course because of *The Compromise*.

However, I consider my life worth nothing to me; my only aim is to finish the race and complete the task the Lord Jesus has given me—the task of testifying to the good news of God's grace.

—Acts 20:24 (NIV)

YOU ARE WORTH IT

GROWING UP I lived in and out of motels, cars, and shelters. I attended seven different schools, and lived in three different states. My mother typically went where the drugs were, and did whatever it took to pay for them.

> I was sucked in by a guy's desire to give me attention.

I was in seventh grade when we moved to Reno, Nevada. I didn't have many friends in Washington where I'd spent the first half of my life, so I was excited about the move. I had been picked on and tortured in grade school mostly for being poor and on welfare. We moved around a lot and making new friends wasn't easy. Most days I didn't want to go to school because of the bullying.

My mother's addictions and lifestyle were what led to me meeting my twenty-four-year-old boyfriend, when I was only twelve years old.

It was at a halfway house for recently-released convicts, who hung out at the motel room we called "home." At such a young age, I was not privy to information like criminal histories—I was sucked in by a guy's desire to give me attention.

By age thirteen I had moved in with him, and things became different quickly. It was like being a real adult—I loved the freedom of living with

91

I was fourteen years old the first time I entered the local pregnancy clinic.

him. What teen girl wouldn't like having no rules, no bedtime, no curfew, and eating whatever, whenever she wanted? With this newfound freedom, being in a relationship with an older man, I could have things I never dreamed of having. He bought me expensive shoes and clothes, and even my first car. We had our own home, which I got to decorate and make mine. These were all things I never had. He also brought feelings of stability, love, and security. Something else I never had. I felt as though I didn't have a care in the world. To me life couldn't get any better.

I began to love my new school, made a lot of friends, and started to have a real passion for sports. In Washington, I couldn't afford most sports, and when I could, I was picked on so badly I wouldn't join a team. Suddenly, I loved them all and wanted to try them all! I even defied the odds and joined the wrestling team, although the guys on the team were less than thrilled about it.

Although I was doing well, I still made a few bad choices. I skipped school occasionally to smoke weed and cigarettes. I really didn't party, but I loved hanging out with my friends and laughing about the dumb stuff in life.

My mother and sisters lived in and out of different motels on one of the worst streets in Reno. That area was filled with drugs, prostitution, and the homeless. I felt safe with a man to protect me, and a place to call home.

The more I stayed away from my mother's transient lifestyle, the more my confidence blossomed. Moving had finally given me a new chance to reinvent myself. My mother was not only a drug user, but was also very abusive mentally and physically. My sisters and I endured it all; we saw it all. I didn't know my biological father but at the same time, it was of no importance to me. All I felt I needed was my boyfriend. We could start our own family and I could do it better than my parents had done.

I was fourteen years old the first time I entered the local pregnancy clinic. I was nervous and a little excited because I was certain I was pregnant. I knew I had missed taking my birth control pills, and we weren't using back-up protection. The doctor came in and confirmed what I already knew. I was pregnant! I walked out of the clinic more nervous than I walked in. How was I going to tell my mother? How was I going to tell anyone?

I was certain everyone would condemn me when they heard the news: "You're too young." "He's too old." "You guys aren't even married yet." As I sat on the bus going home, I looked around in paranoia that people could already tell and were judging me. However, the longer I sat on the bus, the more I realized that there wasn't any way those who knew my living situation could have thought this wasn't going to happen sooner or later. I went home that day and told my boyfriend and a few friends. I was already three months pregnant. I had a lot to worry about and a lot for which to prepare. I didn't have time to take a chance that my mother would ruin my pregnancy with her negativity, so I did my best to hide it from her for as long as possible.

I was very slender, about eighty-nine pounds and not much meat on my bones. My size made it hard for me to hide my growing belly. Despite past difficulties with my mother, I saw her on a daily basis, but was able to cover things up with big sweatshirts and overalls.

Along the way, she had met someone and decided to get married for the third time. While preparing for the wedding, I was forced to have a dress fitting. After that, there was no hiding my growing waistline and she commented, "you either have an eating disorder or you're pregnant!" She immediately purchased a pregnancy test and of course, now six months along, it was positive.

Even though I knew by the kicking and rapid movement in my tiny round belly that a baby was definitely in there, a huge sense of relief came over me to see that plus sign again. I hadn't seen a doctor yet, but I read everything I could find about how to care for myself to keep the baby healthy. I was eating right, and taking prenatal vitamins I purchased from the local pharmacy. I walked every day, and counted kicks. It helped me not only understand my body, but also started me off wanting to be healthy so I could have a healthy baby.

My mother took me straight to the hospital to make sure the baby was healthy and get an approximate due date based on the ultrasound. I only had a little piece of paper the clinic gave me that was a guess based on my last period and a little circle pinwheel. I felt it was not the most accurate, but to my surprise, it was pretty close. I was filled with joy when the ultrasound confirmed that I was having a beautiful baby girl. As I watched the monitor, I could see my baby girl suck her thumb and kick around. I felt relieved and excited. I also felt a little guilty for not seeing a doctor sooner, but I was there now and felt like everything would be okay.

In the wake of all this joy, a bomb was suddenly dropped on my life. One night as I slept, there was a knock at the door. My boyfriend jumped up and as he moved towards the door, I heard a police radio. His parole officer was there to do a check in. It was around two in the morning. I stood there a little confused and sleepy as the female officer began questioning me about being there. I realized this may have been trouble looking me straight in the face, and now that I was pregnant, I had to come up with a story. There was no way I was going back to my mother's motel room to raise my child. I wanted more for my precious baby, and my boyfriend was the one who had it to offer.

I lied and said my mother and I had a fight and she allowed me to stay the night so I didn't roam the streets, pregnant. The officer called my mother to confirm my story. My heart dropped when I overheard the parole officer express her concern that my boyfriend had been in prison for attempted murder of his ex-girlfriend, and he did it right in front of his five children. I was in complete shock! However, my mother continued to reassure the officer that I was in the best possible place for the night. My mother went on to tell her she didn't want to cause a fight that would cause stress to the baby, and she trusted him. The parole officer seemed semi-satisfied, but still had a look of concern on her face. She silently shook her head and walked out, keys shaking on her hip with every step she took.

With this new information about my boyfriend's past, my mother now had more leverage on me than ever, and her plan was to use it to her full advantage. If she wanted cigarettes, we better go and get them. If her room rent was due, she would require us to pay, or threaten to call the police if we didn't. She was a master in the art of manipulation.

On top of being on edge and living in constant fear of my mother's threats, my relationship began to become unhinged. My boyfriend became controlling about what I wore, where I went, and to whom I spoke. Then the physical abuse started.

One night I got up from the bed with the sudden urge that every nine-month pregnant woman has. I had to pee, and I had to pee *now!* I ran to the bathroom and after I was done, washed my hands and headed toward our bedroom. My boyfriend was hiding behind the door like a predator ready to pounce. He tackled me, forced me to the bed, and held me down by the throat. He began screaming at me, saying I was a whore and that I left to cheat on him. He smacked me across the face. It burned my cheek and broke my heart. How could he do this to the mother of his child? My mind quickly raced back to the conversation the probation officer and my mother had over the phone. Did he actually have the ability to kill me? I was afraid once again of being beaten, but this time by him, not my mother. As I lay there, he ripped my shorts off and began to check me for any physical signs of me cheating. When I tried to move, he slammed me down and screamed at me. I lay there motionless and fearful of what was to come next.

After he was done, he threw my shorts at my face. As I cautiously slid them back on, I cried silently to myself, feeling completely violated. He wasn't fazed a bit. He simply lay back down, grumbling under his breath, and fell back to sleep.

There was no sleep for me that night. Or the next. Rubbing my belly, tears streaming down my face, I lay there, sad and scared, knowing what he was capable of. I had no feeling of protection—my stability and security were gone. Yet I had nowhere else to turn.

That summer, I began the first day at my new school. It was an all girls' school for teen moms. I felt a little tired and stressed with the baby's due date just around the corner. The night of August 29, I couldn't sleep and the pain was unbearable. I tossed and turned, took a bath, and did all I could to stop it. I was dehydrated a few times during my pregnancy so I awakened several times during the night to drink lots of water, and then rock and cry myself back to sleep.

On August 30, at four o'clock in the morning, I woke up to try and get my daily "duties" done. I made my boyfriend's lunch and cleaned the house as I usually did. I went to the bathroom to pee with the full intention that after I was done with my cleaning and he left for work, I was going straight back to bed. Those plans changed very quickly.

While I was in the bathroom, I noticed that there was blood; my heart began to race with worry. I screamed for my boyfriend and when he entered the bathroom, I showed him the blood. We grabbed my bag and rushed to the hospital. I was terrified something was wrong.

As I checked into labor and delivery, my boyfriend called my mother and my sisters. Somehow, the news also traveled to my old school, and within minutes, the hospital was filled with teens, teachers, my sisters, my mother, and her new husband. I had done a tour of the hospital a few weeks earlier. I remembered the nurse telling me that the showers were available to use when in labor. I jumped at the chance to soothe my pain. The doctor came in to check on me, looked over my charts, and asked questions. She explained that the blood I saw was my "bloody show" and that the baby could come any time between now and two weeks. A little disappointed, I nodded in agreement and asked what I should do now. Since my water hadn't broken, she told me they would watch me for a couple more hours, check my progress and see if I was dilating, and if nothing happened, she would release me. She left and there I sat rubbing my large belly, feeling like this was the day, and there was no way I was going home.

After hours of sitting in the shower, pain- and stress-free, she told me she wanted me to get out so that she could check and see how dilated I was. The minute I stepped out of the shower, the pain returned full force. She began to check me and said that my bag was dripping and that she was going to rupture it with a thin stick similar in looks to a crochet needle.

My daughter entered the world exactly one hour later at seven pounds three ounces, and nineteen inches long. She was perfect! I held her for a brief moment, and then she was taken for examination by her pediatrician.

As I lay in the recovery room, my mother came in shortly after my boyfriend left to talk to me about what it would mean to put my boyfriend's last name on the birth certificate. She said that if the police found out, my daughter would quickly be removed from my custody. This meant she would legally be fatherless, but I was so afraid they would take her, I decided it was the best choice for now. She then told me how her new marriage was falling apart and she wanted *her* husband's last name on the birth certificate in an attempt to convince him to stay with her. I was confused at this request and to be honest, I was enraged. If their marriage was so bad, I was concerned that if they did divorce it would mean that my daughter would be stuck with that last name. He wasn't even her true family. I told her it was a very big deal and I needed rest before we could discuss it any further. I already knew my answer, but didn't have the energy to fight with her just then. She left it at that and I fell asleep.

When I awakened, my daughter's birth certificate papers were filled out and turned in. I couldn't believe it! She did it anyway. She completed my daughter's birth certificate with her husband's last name. Her actions were morally wrong; I didn't consent to any of it. It also happened to be illegal. I immediately called for a nurse, but before she could reach my room, my mother advised me of the consequences of alerting them to the scam. The sinking feeling in my stomach was of hopelessness and fear. She was adding to the leverage she already had, but now she was using the love of my daughter as emotional blackmail.

My first day back to school was only two weeks after I gave birth to my baby girl. A woman came to our school shortly after my return to share information about a new Christian teen mom program called YoungLives that was starting in our area. She was so full of joy and wore a huge cheerful smile on her face the entire time she was there. Every person I had around me growing up was not that way at all, so I thought she was pretty weird.

Later she called me a few times leaving very "peppy" voicemails about the first club meeting, and explained there would be free diapers and other teen moms there. I decided to attend only for the free diapers. Within moments of showing up, I felt a renewed hope and an excitement for life grow inside me. I saw it in the other moms too. I got to be a teen again. We laughed and played the silly games I never got to play in my life. My daughter was taken care of by women who enjoyed holding and loving babies, so I had a couple of hours to myself. I felt safe and secure. They donated their time to bring joy to my daughter and me. When I expressed gratitude, they told me "*You are worth it.*"

Things continued getting rockier with my mother. She asked me to put my daughter on food stamps under her name. I didn't understand how she could ask me to do that. I was not going to let her put my child on state assistance so she could reap the benefits. My baby was no paycheck. I had let this go on for far too long and I was going to stand my ground.

One afternoon, I brought my daughter over to my mother's motel. It was a hot day, so I dressed my baby in a onesie and socks and wrapped her in a light receiving blanket. When we arrived, my mother handed me a baby outfit. I looked at her with a very puzzled look on my face, curious why she left the receipt attached. Snatching it back in anger, she said, "What's the deal? You bring my grandchild over with no clothes on, I give you a $5 outfit, and you're upset?" she snarled.

I snapped back, "Why did you leave the receipt? I don't care how much it cost. It was the thought that counted."

She quickly announced I was to pay her back. Rolling my eyes and grabbing my things to leave, she grabbed my baby. I didn't want any trouble and I had not come for this drama. I demanded she give my daughter back. She took off out of the room and ran to another motel room. I screamed in horror and frantically tried to get her to stop. One of my sisters was behind me and I felt my body slam to the ground knocking the wind out of me. I had no idea what was going on. A chair slammed behind me and I remember being flung into it.

I was still gasping for air when she returned without my little girl. She began smacking me, telling me what a bad mother I was, and that I was not getting my baby back. "How dare you bring her in public with no clothes on!" I felt her rip at my hair and hold my head back as I screamed for her to give me my daughter. Another sting of her hand across my face over and over again. This was bad, very bad. I was trapped. All I wanted was my baby and we would go about our day and pretend none of this ever happened. She was intent on keeping her.

I quickly grabbed my phone and hit speed-dial for my boyfriend. She snatched the phone away, and told him I was irresponsible and had the baby out with no clothes on. She let him know in a firm tone that she would not endanger that child by giving her back to me. He headed straight there with not another word. By the time he arrived I had taken all the beating I could and sat limp in the chair crying, "Please, give me my baby back, just please give me my baby back!" Tears, blood, and sweat stuck to my face, exhaustion written on me from head to toe. He finally convinced her that he would "handle it" and she returned the baby to his care giving me the death look as he grabbed my hand to help me up.

Christmas time finally arrived and I was excited to leave Reno and head to Visalia where my boyfriend's mother and family lived. My mother pleaded with me one more time to please let her put my baby on her food stamps, and I respectfully declined.

We headed out, driving through the night to make it there for Christmas. We enjoyed our time away from Reno and my mother's demands. I learned how to make tamales and menudo for the first time. I sat and talked with his sister many nights about my worries and fears. We were the same age and although she didn't have a child, she understood me. I explained how I overheard the conversation the parole officer had with my mother and asked if it was true. She confirmed it, and said he had five children. They were all adopted out after he stabbed their mother in the eye, right in front of the children, after finding her with drugs and another man. I felt a little more secure since I knew I would never do that, so hopefully he would never harm me as badly as he had his ex-girlfriend. We packed up our truck just after New Year's and headed back to Reno.

Monday morning I went to school, checked my daughter into childcare, and sat at my desk. I don't remember how far into the day we were when a woman asked me to join her in the hallway. She had me follow her across the street where the main office was. I noticed police cars in the parking lot and hoped it wasn't what I thought it was.

It was exactly that—my mother had finally done it. She'd called the police. However, what she reported was so farfetched from what I thought she would tell them. The police began questioning me about my boyfriend and said that my mother reported me as a runaway; that my boyfriend was now holding me captive in his home and raping me; and that I just had a child from the alleged rape. She went too far! I told the officers what really happened, that my mother knew exactly where I was and that she consented to our relationship. She was merely upset because I wouldn't let her put my daughter on welfare for her benefit.

They advised me to choose my words wisely—I had just turned fifteen, and this was a crime.

The next set of events was a blur. My daughter was taken from me and my boyfriend was arrested. Our home was seized and thoroughly searched. All the drawers dumped, cabinets emptied, a complete disaster. Our once cute little home was completely ravaged.

I was taken to a shelter for foster children where my princess was placed. Instead of going over to the teen side, I begged and pleaded for them to let me be with her. Every day I was watched like a hawk, but I didn't care, I just wanted to be with my baby. I wasn't allowed to do anything with her without their permission but they put a bed for me next to her crib. Every thirty minutes throughout the night, a bright light would flash into my face and I had to acknowledge them for verification I hadn't taken off with her. I had to log every time I fed her, and every time I changed her, or put eczema cream on her dry skin. Our whole life was now charted and filed, watched and recorded.

We had our day in the courtroom and the judge was kind enough to let me speak on my behalf as to where I was to go. He told me if I chose to move back with my mother, I would have to give her parental rights to my daughter. If I chose to stay in foster care, he would allow me physical custody but not parental rights until I was of legal age.

As much as it hurt, I knew my answer. "I grant parental rights to the state of Nevada, sir," I said. I'd die before I'd allow my mother to see or touch my baby again.

I asked the judge if I could say one more thing, and he agreed.

"Sir, my sisters are in grave danger. That woman is not a good mother and has beaten us since we were children. They won't admit it because she has threatened us before about reporting her drug use and abuse, but please take my word, they are in danger." I pleaded to him. It didn't seem to faze a soul in there except my mother. I stared her straight in the eyes and spoke those words. I wanted her to know: "You don't scare me anymore. What's wrong is wrong."

Then the police investigation of my boyfriend continued. I showed and told the police where they could find plenty of evidence that my mother had made a false report. She lied again, like so many other times she did in the past. The police found Christmas cards, pictures of him and me at her wedding and family BBQs. There was so much proof, they couldn't ignore it.

My mother escaped charges, and my sisters being taken from her, by running away to Idaho. The evidence found saved my boyfriend from a lot of jail time. He did spend six months in prison for violating parole, but the rest of the charges were dropped.

After a few months in the foster care center, I finally found a foster home that would take both my daughter and me. We settled in, but at the same time, my boyfriend was being released from prison. My foster mother met him and granted me permission to be with him after school, but I had to be home every night…and no sex! After a short stay in her home, my social worker found my biological father, and he drove from California to meet his long lost daughter and granddaughter. We sat and talked about school and life. I told him how I was ready to get out of foster care and marry my boyfriend. I also told him that my boyfriend already talked to my mother and after a $1,500 negotiation, she signed the papers needed to make it legal. My father told me he wanted to pay for our wedding since he had not been around. So that week, in a little chapel, dressed in black, I was married! Deep in my heart, I knew this was the beginning of the end, but I didn't feel like I had any other option.

Shortly after we were married, I began working a full-time job at a sandwich shop and attended full-day high school at an alternative school. It worked out great because there was childcare right in the school. It wasn't segregated like the all-girls school that made being a teen mom feel like it was a disease and they didn't want us to give it to anyone else. At the school I attended, there were teen moms, teen dads, and "regular" teens.

My biggest troubles came my junior year of high school. I was on the dance team and my dance partner and I were practicing for the first recital of the year with our team. As he spun me around and we transitioned in place for the song change, my husband walked in. We had a closed campus, so immediately my dance teacher told him to leave.

He walked straight up to my dance partner with rage in his eyes. My husband stood 5'3" and my partner was a good 5'7" and they stared each other down. Everyone felt a fight coming. My dance teacher was a tiny blonde woman and was already locking the school down on code red. She had sheer panic on her face and ran stumbling over every chair in the lunchroom to get to the phone. I didn't know whom I was more afraid for as their eyes stayed locked and words were exchanged.

Luckily my husband made it out of the school before the police arrived. The vice principal of the school was willing to let him go if he stayed off school property and caused no more trouble for the students ever again.

When I got home that day, my husband beat me until I was black and blue. He disconnected the battery from my car, shut my phone off, and forbade me to see anyone. He "sentenced me to home confinement" until I could learn to stop being a "whore." He threw a DVD at me from across the room and it sliced my forehead open. I could never tell anyone about my abuse—I was so ashamed and afraid of losing my husband. I had an insane thought stuck in my head that my daughter would hate me later if I couldn't make things work with her daddy.

When I didn't show up for school for a week, my dance partner and his brother came searching for me. After an unrelenting interrogation session, I told them everything I had been going through. They were two of five people I confided in during those brutal times. Some people watched as he smacked me down to the ground in front of them but never spoke a word. My husband became more and more dangerous. I was not going to school as much; I lost my spot on student council, and he forbade me from doing any of the other activities that I loved.

I secretly began to drink a lot and started doing drugs to numb my pain. I was desperately searching for a way to escape my life. I tried a couple of times to commit suicide by taking a lot of Tylenol. His controlling and abusive ways were getting to be too much and I just couldn't take it anymore. He began sleeping with everyone I knew, just to hurt my feelings. Anytime I offended him, spoke up to defend myself, or made him angry, he would take the battery out of my car, shut my phone off, and lock me in the house. He wouldn't let me go to school and sometimes he wouldn't even let me eat. He would hold all his money over my head and made me quit my job so I had no separate income. The only thing he ever let me do was go to the Christian teen mom program I had been going to off and on since I first had my daughter because it was all girls.

With all the struggles and pain in my life, the talks I heard about God didn't make a lot of sense to me. My husband allowed me to spend a weekend at a Christian camp that was just for teen moms. My time there was a place of relief and friendship. It was a safe place where I could laugh and be silly. There was no judgment or drama, just fun and friends. Whenever it would come to a part where a leader would stand up and talk about Jesus, I would count squares on the walls, go to the bathroom, braid my hair, talk, text, anything to get out of listening to what I felt was a false hope. Something I felt I was not worthy of—yet time after time I would hear the leaders tell me, *"You are worth it."*

How could anyone love me the way they told me this Jesus guy did? My life was such a mess!

It wasn't until my second year at camp that I really got it. As the speaker stood there and spoke, my heart soaked it all in and began to soften. Jesus spoke right to my heart and said, *"You are worth it, I love you and I will never leave you."* I sat there for fifteen minutes and drank in the unfamiliar feelings of warmth and joy. There was so much comfort in that moment! It was the same information my YoungLives leaders had been telling me for years, but this time I really received it.

With overwhelming feelings and tears streaming down my face, I accepted Jesus, and couldn't wait to continue living my life with Him in it.

YoungLives continued to be a place for me to escape my mess. All of my friends went so it was a great place to go and be with them. A place to be me. A place I felt safe. I loved my leaders and after my second year at camp, they embraced me in my new life choice to know Jesus. I went to church with the leaders. I had dinner with their families and joined them for movie nights. I loved watching Christian women be silly, fun, and amazing moms. I'd never seen this in my life, and had a much-distorted vision in my head of what a Christian woman looked like. They broke all of the stereotypes quickly and showed me being a Christian wasn't boring.

I kept my home life very private. Not only was I afraid for my own safety, but also anyone else that knew about my husband's abuse. Not many people ever stood up to him.

My baby girl saw things that no child should ever see and it opened my eyes to how badly we needed to leave.

One summer morning, I woke up to make breakfast, clean, and get my husband's lunch ready, just like I always did. I don't remember what happened exactly, but there was something very wrong in his eyes. I knew I would be in trouble when he returned home—however, fear made me stay. I'd left many times before, stayed in motels, stayed with friends, or even a few leaders' homes. I was tired of running, and I thought maybe I could talk to him and try to fix it.

When he got home that night, he said I was cheating and I would pay. My husband forced me to have sex with him even though I begged him to stop. Then he beat and tortured me for days. At one point, he placed a gun in my mouth, while ripping my hair out, and told me it would be the last time I took a breath.

I had small moments of relief when he would stop to think of his next move. My daughter was two years old at this time and sat watching as her daddy abused her mommy. The only thing that stopped him was her small voice coming around the corner as he cocked the gun back. She screamed at him to stop. Her exact words are etched into my mind, "No, Daddy, pwease stop pweease." He released me and told me to stay in my room. I realized then that if something didn't change, my child and I could end up dead one day. My baby girl saw things that no child should ever see and it opened my eyes to how badly we needed to leave.

He arranged for his sister to travel from Visalia to Reno to help him with our daughter. She arrived before I awakened one morning, and sat in the living room chair, by the front door. I was in prison and she was my warden. Did he invite her to come help because he had plans to kill me? I returned to my room and closed the door. I was about to break into tears, feeling lost and hopeless and in that moment, I felt Jesus pick up my chin and help me gain the last ounce of strength I had to fight for my child and myself.

I quietly pulled the window open and climbed out. I walked over to my neighbor's house to call for help. I was overwhelmed with fear as

I knocked on her front door, and I think she could see it in my eyes. I told her I really needed to use the phone, I was being held against my will, and my daughter was still inside. She already knew all of it, she could hear everything through the walls of her apartment, but was always afraid to interfere. She wrapped me in a hug and apologized.

I called the one person I knew I could trust, but was afraid to tell my secret to: my YoungLives leader. I cried as I told her I was keeping this from her for so long for fear of disappointing her. She assured me she was not mad at me and that I needed to get to safety. She gave me instructions to go back and pack what I could and she would be there. I was so afraid because I knew he had guns and he told his sister to not let me leave.

I did as she told me, and twenty minutes after I made the call, she arrived at my house.

She knocked on the door and politely asked for me. My husband's sister told her I could not leave until she could call her brother. My YoungLives leader gave a sweet smile, and I watched in awe as passion and fire started rising up in her eyes, and she said, "I can take them now without any trouble or we can get the police."

She swooped up my daughter as I grabbed the couple bags I was able to pack of her clothes. She got us safely into her minivan that had transported us so many times to club and camp. I could see the fear in her face but she remained calm and collected for all of us. She knew that my husband knew where she lived and was afraid it was the first place he would come to find us. To assure our safety she took us to her mom's new home.

She asked me where I could go that I wouldn't be found and I wouldn't easily go back to him. The only place I knew was in Washington where I spent the first half of my life. She did some research and unfortunately found out that it was illegal for me to leave with his child without giving him my new address and phone number within twenty-four hours. So we planned it out for me to call and tell him once I was far enough ahead that he wouldn't catch up.

Within hours, I had a bus ticket for the two of us to travel to Washington. Without goodbyes to my friends, I stepped onto the bus bound for a safer place, and a new life.

We traveled all night and all day until arriving in the state of Washington. A friend picked me up from the bus station in Tacoma. I met a man on the bus and discovered we both lived a couple blocks from each other. I embraced him in a hug before we left, and was grateful for his friendship.

I lived in a homeless shelter until I could apply for housing and get on my feet. I was approved about a month later. My husband would call me and tell me awful things to break my spirit. He would tell me everyone he had cheated on me with during our marriage, and that he had fathered several of my friends' children.

I continued my friendship with the guy I met on the bus, and he became a huge support. He would listen to my anger-filled rants and give advice when he could. We quickly grew closer to each other and started a relationship.

We began living together, and three months after I moved into my new home, I was pregnant again.

During my pregnancy, I was determined to finish high school, and did. I then enrolled myself into college, with Sociology as my major, and started to think of what a better future would look like for my children and me. I continued to talk to my YoungLives leader on a daily basis. She encouraged me and offered me wisdom.

I was blessed with a handsome son. Yet life still seemed off track. I soon realized my son's father had some issues of his own, but also was a huge part in helping me through mine. We talked a lot about my abusive relationship with my ex-husband. He ultimately let me vent about it until there was not as much anger and hurt in my heart. A saying I've heard that brings me comfort is: "*God puts people in our lives for a reason, a season, or a lifetime. When they have accomplished the purpose He's placed them in your life for, you must move forward without them, peacefully.*"

He saw his son once after he was born. We intended to maintain our friendship, but his inability to fight his addictions kept us far apart. It was a gift though. I learned my lesson about heading down that path. I was now eighteen years old and a single mother of two.

I started my first real job at AmeriCorps with six other young women. They helped mold me into a bold, brave, semi-funny, and loud woman. One friend in particular helped me pick up my kids from daycare every day, then clean, cook, and shop. She even helped me see that my life really is nothing without God. She taught me if I could just see God in everything I accomplished and give Him all the glory, I could live my life to the fullest. She also invited me to join her and take my kids to church occasionally.

We became very close, and gave each other a hand up when we would fall.

I started reading a book called *A Purpose-Driven Life,* which I received from my YoungLives leader before I left Reno. I was growing in my faith, and learning that every single seed planted in YoungLives was beginning to bloom. I was beginning to heal, find hope, and dream again.

Through mutual friends, I met an amazing man about a year later.

God continued His work in me, walking me down the path of healing, teaching me to forgive, and to do that seventy times seven (like the Bible says) every time the memories I could never erase returned to haunt me. When I met this amazing man, there was something different about him. I saw something I hadn't seen before in a man's eyes. I saw a southern gentleman with a passion for Christ. A loving man who was kind, funny, and adventurous. He complemented me, and my personality, in every way.

This was something I had never known when it came to men. He challenged me every day to see God. To be thankful for each blessing, even if they didn't seem like blessings to me in that moment. He intrigued my heart and soul. God sent this man to me; He sent him to my children.

It has been eight years since I met this incredible man and seven since we've been married. We had our dream wedding with the white gown, in a church, with family and friends by our sides. Happiness and joy filled every corner of the room! My YoungLives leader and her husband flew in from Reno. My uncle and my YoungLives leader's husband both walked me down the aisle. We now have three beautiful children. We are a family that loves the Lord and understands that He has a divine plan for us. We keep Him in the center of our lives. We know His love is unfailing, never ending, and unconditional. I know that every hard time I walked through was *worth it.*

I now have a testimony that will change the lives of other women, offer them hope, remind them they are not alone, and tell them, *You are worth it.*

I had the privilege a directing a YoungLives ministry that we started in Arizona and watched it grow from three teen moms to thirty-five in just three years.

We then traveled 2,400 miles from my first ministry in Arizona to begin another one in Indiana! God called me to spread the word further and continue impacting lives.

God then brought everything full circle as He guided me home to Reno, where I got to restart the very YoungLives ministry I started in so many years ago. The exact place where my life was forever changed!

I realize now that it was all intentional! I now understand the reason the weird woman who entered my school years ago was so happy. She knew what it felt like to be fully loved by Jesus, free of guilt, and to understand God as a Father who would never leave. Her joy was in sharing that with teen moms, and the rest of the world.

I now know that joy and get to share it with other teen moms. It truly is a blessing to be able to see God work in the lives of these girls and their precious babies! Transforming generations and breaking cycles.

My mess became my *message!*

If you are a teen mom or about to be a teen mom, be encouraged and know that you are able to overcome things you never thought you could, go further than you thought your feet could ever take you, and see Jesus in those moments! He is real and will never leave you or forsake you. He is a Father to the fatherless and loves you with an unending love.

To the YoungLives leaders reading this: Please know that most of you will never get to see this kind of story evolve. Don't let that discourage you as you grow with the teen moms you're working with. It took me almost seven years to see what my leaders meant, to really understand the funny skits, colorful wigs, the scuba fins at the bowling alley, the pies in the faces, and the measuring of local buildings with hot dogs. When it clicked though, it really clicked.

If you happen to be a parent of a teen mom, a teacher, or even just a friend helping her on her journey, remember this:

Every step you take with her will not only be imperative to her path now but also later on in life, as she reflects on her adventure.

Put your trust in God and He will *not* fail you

Every tear you wipe, every hand you lend, and every diaper you change will show her the kind of love that Jesus has to offer her and her baby.

It will give her hope, inspire her to dream, and cover her with love that every person should have bestowed upon them in life.

Not every challenge will be easy—some will probably be way beyond your capacity to control or understand. Your display of strength and composure will go far, and set an example for not only one but future generations as well.

I'm still in constant contact with the YoungLives leader that was so pivotal in transforming my life so many years ago. My kids call her and her husband grandma and grandpa, and they are like parents to me. I couldn't thank them more for really showing me what Jesus' love truly looks like. It's been completely unconditional! They walked through life with me, hard times and good times. They stood in the pool with me, holding my hand at my baptism, and were there on my wedding day. We visit back home when we can, but always remember to call and exchange pictures. I can hear her words ring in my ear from so many years ago reminding me daily, "*You are worth it.*"

It doesn't matter if you are a teen mom, a teacher, a social worker, or a YoungLives leader. Love like Jesus' always helps you stand tall, when you feel all is lost. Put your trust in God and He will *not* fail you, no matter how far you've fallen, no matter what you've gone through or done. Jesus will always reach out His hand and say, "I do love you and I will never leave you, because *you are worth it!*"

For I am the LORD your God who takes hold of your right hand and says to you, Do not fear; I will help you.

—Isaiah 41:13 (NIV)

IT WAS DIFFERENT

MY PARENTS WORKED a lot! Our family owned a winery in Salem, Oregon, and running this family business seemed all-consuming.

My parents divorced when I was five. They remained friendly so that made things a little easier but it was still hard to grow up that way. My mom moved my older sister and me to Yakima, Washington, which was over four hours away from my father. She bought a home with another man and together they had boy, girl twins.

His family never seemed to accept my mom, my sister, or me. Holidays made this painfully obvious when the twins were flooded with presents and we got little or nothing, or at least that's how it seemed. They were mean to my mom and her boyfriend never stood up for her. We were not accepted as family.

When my new siblings came along, I became the middle child. I often felt lonely and forgotten. My older sister was loud and opinionated, and the twins were difficult to manage. My mom was basically a single mom, receiving little help from her boyfriend. I seemed to get by on my own, got good grades, had lots of friends, and played sports.

I enjoyed the frequent trips to visit my dad. Now that my parents were separated, he seemed to be able to focus on being present when we were with him. He took care of most of our wants. He took us shopping, bought us candy and pop, video game systems, and we just generally had fun. It was difficult for my mom to unwind us once we came back home. She had much more on her plate with the extra kids and couldn't afford to provide all the cool stuff my dad could.

After six years of living in Yakima, my mom's relationship with her boyfriend became rocky. He left and took both of our cars with him. We were left alone and stranded.

Within days, my dad became a super hero. He showed up at our house with a very nice minivan, dropped it off, and rode the Greyhound bus home. He always seemed to make sure we were taken care of.

I never really understood how bad our financial situation was. My mom was always good about keeping that part of our life pretty well hidden. She didn't want us to carry that burden. I knew we were on food stamps and that wasn't good. However, I never went without. One day I stayed home sick from school so I had to take a trip to Seattle with my mom for a meeting about our home. I waited in the car. I could tell it hadn't gone well when my mom returned to the car fighting back tears. I told her I was hungry and asked if we could get something to eat. She searched the car for a snack on the floor or the seat back pocket. I was so confused why we couldn't just go get something at a restaurant since that's what we would have typically done. I could see the conversation bringing more tears to my mom's eyes as she tried to explain in a way I could understand that we just couldn't afford to.

I realize this may sound crazy, but just then, a $20 bill floated down from the bridge overhead, right to where we were. We were in shock, excited, and relieved. The tears ended and together we enjoyed a hot lunch. From that moment on, my mom seemed to have more hope that whatever we were facing, we would get through it.

Through the years, we've had many incredible blessings, but that one was undoubtedly from God. *It was different.*

When I was twelve, my dad became a hero once again. My mom had no way to pay the mortgage on our home. My dad stepped in to help and covered the payment so my mom could get the house sold.

We moved back to the Salem area with very little money. My older sister remained in Yakima. My mom, my two younger siblings, and I moved into a small one-bedroom apartment that my dad built above the winery. My parents remained friendly with each other and had always been better business partners than spouses.

Making the right choice felt lonely.

This season of my life was difficult. I was forced to try and make new friends at thirteen years old when most have already been formed. I had to leave a lot of great friends behind in Yakima and couldn't seem to make similar close friendships in Salem. The friends I did make I couldn't invite over for sleepovers because of the size of our home and I didn't tell anyone what our living situation was like.

My mom and dad both worked long hours. I remained active in sports. However, my parents were rarely able to attend my sporting events. My soccer coach would drive me home from practice and games, dropping me off at the winery with a questioning look on his face. "Do your parents always work this late?" I always had a story so I wouldn't have to tell him we were living there. I was so embarrassed by it! It wasn't a bad living situation, but *it was different.*

Entering high school, I was insecure and self-conscious. I had a few friends, but none of them seemed to be a very good influence. I went through the motions: going to class, turning in my work, being as involved as I could, but my heart wasn't in it. These were not the "best years of your life" as I'd heard so many people say. I watched, as friends would smoke pot, but thought they were stupid and looked stupid when they were high. Pot eventually led to other drugs, and I remained an outsider because I chose not to get involved. I slowly began to lose friendships. One of them became pregnant and moved in with her boyfriend. Others just went their separate ways because of my choice to stay away from drugs. Making the right choice felt lonely.

I was seventeen and a senior in high school. I had good grades and was very active in DECA (Distributive Education Clubs of America). DECA prepares emerging leaders and entrepreneurs in marketing, finance, hospitality, and management in high schools and colleges around the globe. I had hopes of traveling to a national competition and was on track for receiving college scholarships.

Yet all of this wasn't important enough to keep me focused on school. I began to hang out with a girl who was also classified as an "outsider" and we could relate to how each other felt. She was a "wannabe gangsta." We began smoking and skipping school together. She introduced me to older guys who were twenty-two years old. One of them was her manager at McDonalds. The other one I thought was cute! To two seventeen-year-old girls, hanging out with them was "so cool." They were good looking, had parties and their own apartment. We went over there regularly to just hang out. We all got to know each other pretty well. The one that had my attention was funny and outgoing. I was young, naive, and insecure, which made me vulnerable. I knew these were not the best friend choices, but it felt good to have someone to hang out with. I finally had what felt like a close friend again.

My mom was not happy about the time I spent there and tried her best to open my eyes. She did everything she could to pull my head out of the sand as my behavior led me to failing my classes. After I was caught forging notes to skip school, she asked the school to give me every possible punishment they could. Lunch detention, the embarrassment of having to call my mom directly to leave school, and the feeling of failure and disappointment from my teacher when I was removed from DECA, were enough to light a big enough fire under me to fight just hard enough to get my high school diploma. Yet it wasn't enough to make me change my ways. She knew exactly what the road looked like I was headed down. I was blinded by a need for relationship, and I thought *it was different.*

My mom continued her fight to keep me away from my new friends. I had been lonely for too many years to walk away from them. This caused constant fighting between my mom and me. She was always working and when she was home, she focused her time and energy on my younger sister and brother. Due to the lack of a relationship during this time, I didn't listen to her. To try and rein me in, she took my car and so to show her, I moved out. I moved in with a girl that lived across from the guys I had been spending time with, and was the older sister of one of them. My mom called the police to report me as a runaway. However, since I had graduated from high school, and was only a few months away from turning eighteen, they couldn't do anything. This was probably the worst mistake ever!

I graduated in mid-June, moved out right after that, and in late-June started taking classes at the community college. I also got a job at the local mall. The older boy and I started flirting after I turned eighteen. We ended up getting more serious and I moved in with him and his roommate.

Eventually, I learned that he was hot tempered, controlling, and very jealous. He didn't have a job, he smoked a lot of pot, and I am pretty sure he did other things that I was too naive to recognize. Still to this day, I'm not sure why I didn't run as fast and far away as I could when I got the chance. I was blind. I was just a little girl with no self-esteem or self-worth. I seemed to just accept this unhealthy love that I thought I deserved.

Although I was on birth control I had gotten from Planned Parenthood, I was inconsistent with taking it. My periods seemed to always be sporadic, but since I had felt sick for months and was overly bothered by smells that had never bugged me before, I decided to take a pregnancy test. When the test showed positive, I went to Planned Parenthood where they confirmed I was almost four months pregnant.

When I found out I was pregnant, I was emotional and terrified. My boyfriend on the other hand threw a party. He invited all of his friends and got completely wasted and passed around beer and pot. He ran around telling everyone that he was going to be a daddy. He was so happy. I on the other hand, was a mess. Looking back, I realize he acted so happy for show. He wasn't really thinking about all that goes into being a parent whereas I knew my life was changed forever. He still had choices to make. For me, *it was different.*

My boyfriend and I went to my mom's house to tell her together. I remember sitting on the couch facing her and I started to cry. She knew without me saying anything. I remember vividly how I felt because I knew my mom was disappointed in me. She looked sick and scared for me. She never liked my boyfriend and knew he was not kind to me. Now I was stuck with him. I couldn't face my dad so I wrote him a note and left it on his desk. He

> I seemed to just accept this unhealthy love that I thought I deserved.

didn't speak to me for over a month. I knew this would forever change my "daddy's little girl" relationship with my father. From that moment forward, *it was different.*

My boyfriend and I agreed it was time we get our own place and get ready for the baby. We both came from good families so we had a lot of support. His parents were good people and helped us out with furniture and housewares. My mom owned a duplex where my older sister, her boyfriend, and their two-year-old daughter rented one side. She rented the other side to us so we were able to be in our own place that was affordable. I began to work at the family business and my boyfriend bounced around from job to job. He was drinking more and more and dabbling in other drugs. I am not sure of everything he got involved with. I know he eventually got into methamphetamines. This all happened very quickly while I was pregnant. His temper was getting more intense and he treated me terribly. He would spit in my face and yell vulgar things at me. He called me a slut, ugly, and fat, and that's sugar-coating it. I have never heard such terrible things from anyone in my life. He began to get violent. His mood was disjointed along with the ups and downs of drug abuse. My mom's door remained open to me if I ever wanted to go back home. However, now that I was pregnant, I felt stuck, like I had failed, and I fought to make it work. Looking back, I should have run home the first chance I had!

I lost all of my friends other than my close friend who lived a state away. I had very little "teen" time. I was getting ready for a baby. I was trying to fix up the house, painting, and cleaning. I was trying to make a home. My boyfriend wouldn't help with that. He would watch TV or go out with his friends—which I didn't mind, because then I wouldn't have to be around him. I worked during the pregnancy because I was trying to save money and get things the baby needed. My mom began to come around to the idea of me having a baby. She was always supportive of me even though she wasn't thrilled about me having a baby at such a young age. I was scared, but really excited about becoming a mom. It's weird that you don't know until you go through it, but I already loved my baby so much and couldn't wait to meet her. We were poor and relying on my mom for financial help.

I started having contractions late one evening. We went to the hospital thinking I was in labor, but the contractions were too far apart and I wasn't dilated yet so they sent us home. Even though I was still having contractions, I went to work the next day because we needed the money. My boyfriend wasn't working and I couldn't keep up with the bills on my own. That night my contractions got worse. He told me I was being too loud and it was keeping him up so he made me go sleep on the couch. I called my mom and she stayed on the phone with me all night, timing how far apart the contractions were. I was so tired I would fall asleep in between the contractions.

A couple days later, I was back at the hospital. I was in so much pain but it wasn't time for an epidural yet. I hadn't had much sleep since it had been disrupted two nights in a row by contractions. My boyfriend asked the nurse for a cot and slept while telling me to try and be quieter when going through contractions. I felt very alone. My mom and older sister came and helped me through the labor. The labor was long and difficult. My baby girl was stuck in the birth canal for hours, she ingested the amniotic fluid (which is toxic), and the cord was wrapped around her little neck. My sister was filming the delivery and I remember when my daughter finally decided to join the outside world, my mom told my sister to stop filming. My precious baby was blue and not making any sounds or movement. They rushed her off to get her breathing and get the toxic fluid out of her system. I didn't get to hold her until a few hours after she was born.

The moment I finally held my daughter in my arms was indescribable. Holding this gorgeous little bundle of cuteness was the most amazing feeling of my life. It is true that you do not know love until you have a child. I can't explain the absolute joy mixed with absolute fear that takes over in that moment. I just knew I could never love more than I love this child. She was perfect and that moment was beautiful. Every bit of pain was forgotten, and nothing else mattered. At only nineteen years old, I was now a mom to the most beautiful girl in the world.

All I remember about my stay in the hospital was the nurse offering to take my daughter to the nursery so I could get some sleep. I refused. I was exhausted but could not take my eyes off her. This little baby girl enamored me, and she was all mine. My boyfriend had left to go home

> It hadn't been until I had my daughter that I realized that she deserved better and I began to stand up for her and myself.

and get some sleep so it was just my baby and me.

The next few months were nothing short of chaos. My boyfriend continued his ways of drug use, abuse, and affairs. One evening he came home after I had put our daughter to sleep in her crib. He threw the living room chair across the room, breaking it into pieces. He flung the coffee table and called me names. I was afraid to call the police for help with my daughter in the house. I was afraid they would take her from me for allowing her in this environment. I called my mom for help instead, and planned to call the police once my daughter was safely away. Once he heard my phone call, he raced to our daughter's room and picked up my sleeping baby. He held her in his arms and continued yelling at me. I was panicked!

It was as though I got a backbone when I had a baby. It hadn't been until I had my daughter that I realized that she deserved better and I began to stand up for her and myself. She didn't deserve a life with yelling and fighting, hitting and drug addiction. She was so perfect and precious and still is everything to me. Sadly, I didn't realize that I also didn't deserve to be treated that way. The fight I had in me was only for her. I demanded he put her down, and finally he did. I guided him out of her room and locked her door. I had to keep her safe. Finally, my mom and his dad arrived. His dad blamed me for the event that had taken place and my mom demanded that they leave since it was her property.

His parents continued visiting my daughter for several years. They would allow my daughter's father to visit without me being aware of it. He told her things like his girlfriend would be her new mommy. I also learned that he never stopped using drugs. My highest priority was to protect my daughter's innocence, so I ended these visits as well.

This journey has not been easy. It has always been just my daughter and me. Thankfully, my family is close and has always helped. We are surrounded with a lot of love. My mom has always been my rock. She is an amazing grandma and mom. There hasn't been a time that she hasn't been there for my daughter and me. If my baby girl wanted to do dance and I couldn't afford it, my mom would make it happen.

I remained in the duplex and worked at the family business until my daughter was three. Then I got a job working for the state with child welfare. I worked there for three years until my dad got sick and I went back to the family business, where I still work today.

I was on and off with school for years. I graduated with an Associate's degree in human services in 2012. I am still working on my Bachelor's degree in Business Administration.

Over the years, it has been hard to trust for both my daughter and myself. When I find myself letting down my walls to start a relationship, I struggle to take my daughter out of her first place position. I often place her before myself and before any relationship. She has been everything to me for so long that it is extremely difficult to give any energy to anyone else.

My daughter often blames herself for my lost relationships. It is not her fault, and I am learning how to face my struggles. When she doesn't feel good enough because of her dad abandoning her, I tell her that he was not good enough for her. I remind her that he didn't take the time to get to know her, choosing drugs instead, and that if he knew her he would have no choice but to love her because she is that incredible!

We both have a lot to learn and a lot of healing to walk through. It's a daily fight and a choice to let your walls down no matter how hard it is. If you have recently found yourself on this journey of being a teen mom, I encourage you: Don't be afraid to go home. Because of my fear of failure, I faced a lot more trauma by staying and trying to make things work in the chaos. I didn't deserve to be treated that way, and neither do you. Your life is not over. You will get through this. It is hard, but my daughter is the coolest person I know and I wouldn't change my life with her for anything. I am a very blessed mom!

Whether God drops $20 from the sky in your time of need to remind you Jesus is there, or simply walks with you through the trials in your life, Jesus is with you, and

> It's a daily fight and a choice to let your walls down no matter how hard it is.

Jesus is with me. Jesus is truly the only solid, unchanging, fully loving, fully forgiving, and perfect person in existence. I am learning that I am worthy of love and working on letting my walls down. I am ready to be in love, be loved, and eventually get married. I know I am worthy of a healthy relationship but I am willing to wait for the right one. I am learning what perfect love feels like as I learn more about this love that is offered through a relationship with Jesus. In His love I am enough and worthy. I have done my best to love well, but have struggled to feel loved in a relationship. Yet I am learning that with Jesus, I am fully loved. *With Jesus, it is different.*

> *Trust in the LORD with all your heart and lean not on your own understanding; in all your ways submit to him, and he will make your path straight.*
> —Proverbs 3:5-6 (NIV)

A CHANGE

I CAN STILL feel the wintry dread of waking up and having all of my hopes dashed as I remembered the reality of my situation. Life seemed as though it was a bad dream. It was cold and dirty and as much as I wanted to escape, it was my life; it was all I knew. There were four of us kids and my mom constantly struggled to make ends meet. All we had was a wood stove and it never seemed to take the chill out of the house. I was the oldest of four children and was the only one who seemed concerned about the filth we were living in. I would attempt to clean, but it was a daunting task. As soon as one area was cleaned and I tried to move on to the next, my family destroyed the room I had just spent hours cleaning.

My adult life has been spent doing everything possible to escape the trauma I faced as a child. I'm quick to turn the heater on at the slightest hint of a chill and for many years, my house had to be pristine.

My mom was the middle of four children and was left without a father at the age of five. My grandfather abandoned his responsibilities and did his best to distance himself from his kids. My grandmother and her children experienced tremendous struggle. She worked two jobs just to survive, which meant she was gone a lot, leaving my mom and her siblings to fend for themselves. My mom became pregnant with me at the age of seventeen. She married my father and he was there when I was born, but less than a year later, he returned to Mexico for the mandatory waiting period for his green card. He never returned. His departure left a void in my soul that I have spent a lifetime trying to fill.

My mom moved on and became pregnant with my brother when I was about two years old. My brother's father was abusive and I have vivid memories of the fighting. I could do nothing and felt completely helpless. My mom eventually left because she finally had enough. Fortunately, she wasn't married to him. When I was five years old, my mom married again and my sister was born. I watched as my mom played the role of mom and dad because her husband was absent both physically and emotionally. Neither man was a good father figure to me. I was desperate to be cherished by a daddy.

My mind blocked out many of the events that shaped the early years of my childhood. Like an incomplete puzzle, I remembered pieces, but there are gaping holes that I can't seem to fill. I'm not sure my heart could handle the complete picture and I believe that's God's mercy. For instance, I'm aware my great-grandfather was a child molester and I have certain memories that convince me I was likely abused by him. It's as though my mind found a way to protect me and leave out details that may be too disturbing to face. I later found out that my great-grandfather abused most of the grandchildren and potentially some of his own daughters. As I began to uncover the truth, a horrifying reality came to light. The family remained quiet and created a culture of secrets, which enabled him to get away with these atrocities.

Elementary school was torture for me too. I had very few friends and I was taunted and teased relentlessly. At the time, I couldn't understand what was wrong with me but looking back, the cause was obvious. I was a bed-wetter until the age of eight and on top of that, I wasn't taught about hygiene so I had no idea that I reeked of urine. I was an outcast, ostracized for reasons I could not understand. There was something clearly different about me and my peers let me know it. Just to add insult to injury, as I lost my baby teeth, my adult teeth came in with a gap in front. This caused me to be teased even more. My sense of self-worth was stripped from me bit by bit, and day by day.

At the age of twelve, while sleeping over at a family friend's home, my life was changed forever. I was the only girl surrounded by three teen boys. I was getting a lot of attention, which I didn't fully understand. I thought the oldest boy, who was sixteen, was so handsome. I had a crush on him. The boys convinced me to play truth or dare. It started out innocently enough with silly questions and harmless dares but quickly progressed into territory that embarrassed me. I was asked if I was a virgin and for some stupid reason I said I wasn't. They were baiting me but I didn't know it. The dare was to go to the bedroom of the younger brother, who was the same age as I was, and touch him on the arm while he was sleeping. The

> the desperation of wanting the love and attention of a man took precedence over everything else.

sixteen-year-old said he would go with me, so he came and got me sometime in the middle of the night. As we walked down the hall, he guided me into his bedroom. He kissed me and a thrill swept through my body that I'd never known. He began to remove my clothing. I was afraid but I couldn't seem to say no. My innocence was lost that night and I was filled with shame. His last words to me will be forever burned in my mind, "If you get pregnant, get an abortion." I knew then that I had been used. That experience was a deep scar on my soul and I carried it on my journey to find love the rest of my life. I desperately wanted to be loved and accepted. I wanted to be validated and told I was beautiful. I needed a father figure to affirm me.

At the age of thirteen, my stepdad's brothers and cousins came to live with us. They all seemed very nice at first, but I would eventually be coerced into having sex with one of the cousins who was twenty-four years old. I knew what I was doing was wrong, but the desperation of wanting the love and attention of a man took precedence over everything else. Once again, a man used me and I was filled with shame. It wasn't long before I started having stomach cramps. I didn't know what was wrong with me, but I had missed my period. Then the stark reality set in…I was pregnant!

I kept my pregnancy secret until I missed my second period. I knew I had to tell my mom but I was so afraid. When I finally got the courage to tell her, she was very supportive. She told me of her experiences and guided me through my options. She talked about abortion and the pain that comes with it, she expressed her support in raising the baby if I chose to keep it, and she reminded me that my aunt, who really wanted a baby but was unable to have one, could adopt the child. I knew instantly what the right choice was. As I stood in the reality I faced, I knew I couldn't raise a child the way I was raised. I wanted this child to have more; I wanted it to have *a chance.*

My aunt was heartbroken that I was pregnant but at the same time filled with joy to have her dream of having a baby come true. I moved in with her and my uncle shortly after I told my mom I was pregnant. Unfortunately, I shared the news of my pregnancy with a close friend at school and she decided to betray my confidence and share the news with other people. They started asking me if I was pregnant and one boy even told me I was a liar. There were so many whispers. All of the years of taunting and teasing flooded back to me and I plummeted into depression. I stopped attending classes sooner than planned and a tutor came to our home to help me complete eighth grade.

During this time, my uncle began displaying some odd behaviors. He would allow me to see him naked, and justify it by acting as if it was no big deal. He had become the father figure I always wanted so I overlooked his weird behavior. I craved the attention of a man so much that I was willing to do just about anything to preserve it. As I look back now, I know that he was grooming me.

The depression deepened about five months into my pregnancy. Anxiety began to creep in and I wanted to abort the baby even though I knew I was too far along. The cloud around me was so thick and dark that I thought it would literally consume me. I became suicidal but knew I couldn't kill myself because I didn't want to hurt the baby. In my immature mind, I loved the baby but wanted to escape the reality that was mine. I felt so broken, shameful, alone, and confused.

God is the only thing that got me through that time with my sanity intact. I accepted the Lord when I was nine years old and was baptized at Harvest Baptist Church. They had a bus that would come by and pick me up on Sundays. I can't remember if my mom attended my baptism. What I do remember is how sad I was that she didn't attend church with me. We moved shortly after and I was stopped short of knowing how to grow in my new faith.

Fortunately, my aunt was a churchgoer and so I started attending church again when I moved in with her. I started to get to know who

Jesus actually was and my relationship with Him grew. I desired to know Him and He revealed Himself to me in small ways.

> adoption was one of the greatest joys and the greatest traumas all wrapped up into one.

As my pregnancy progressed, I began taking a teen Lamaze class to prepare for the birth. It was in this class that I found some semblance of acceptance. All of the other participants were teen moms too, but I was the youngest by far. I met a woman in that class who mentored me during this desperate time of need. She would pour into me in ways no one else could at the time. She was such a good listener and had a way of communicating with me that made me feel valued and important as an individual. She was not just my doula; she was my angel.

At twenty weeks, the ultrasound showed the baby was a boy. I was grief-stricken knowing I would be giving him away, but I also continued to remind myself that I couldn't give him a good life. I wanted him to have *a chance* to go to college, *a chance* to be free from the burden of poverty, *a chance* to be whatever his heart desired and not to worry about the struggle.

When the time came for him to be born, I was in the hospital surrounded by my aunt, my mom, and my doula. I was terrified, I didn't know what to expect, but my doula kept me calm explaining every step of the process.

I was nearly ripped in two because my body was so tiny. As soon as my son was born, they raised him up, showed him to me, and then he was taken away to bond with my aunt and uncle. All I can remember is how precious he was and how my heart ached when they took him away. His life had ushered forth from my body and it felt surreal. Shortly after, my doula had to leave and my mom left too. I remember lying there, all alone, feeling abandoned, robbed, uncared for, and unimportant. I was naked with nothing but the scars of life, both physically and emotionally. Having a baby at the age of thirteen and giving him up for adoption was one of the greatest joys and the greatest traumas all wrapped up into one.

The biggest blessing was that I was able to return home with my son. My aunt and uncle allowed me to stay with them after his birth. A couple of days after leaving the hospital, I remember laying him on my belly wishing he were inside me again. I had to process all that had happened and grieve not being able to be his mother. So I wrote him a letter, to be delivered on his thirteenth birthday, explaining why I made the choice I did.

I went back to school just a few days after having my son. Lots of kids asked if I was still pregnant since my belly stayed big and I continued wearing maternity clothes. There was another girl in the same grade as me who also had a baby. She talked about how she missed her baby so much while she was at school and expressed her excitement about returning home to be with her daughter. It made me so envious that I questioned my decision about putting my son up for adoption. I felt so empty since I gave my baby away. I got to go home and see him but I didn't get to be his mom.

Two months after I gave birth, my uncle began making weird comments again. I was at my most vulnerable point. I was empty and broken and in desperate need of love. He convinced me to allow him to touch me in my most intimate places. I knew what was happening was wrong, but the sensations and emotions felt so good. These encounters continued for four years, eventually evolving into intercourse. I so badly wanted my son to have a dad that I didn't tell anyone. He was good to the baby and I knew he wouldn't hurt him, so I was able to justify not telling anyone. I had already sacrificed so much to give my child a good life, what was a little more sacrifice? I wanted what was best for my baby no matter the cost to me. I sacrificed myself and laid my life down for him so he would have what I never did.

When my son was nine months old, I learned my aunt and uncle were moving to Portland, Oregon, and I was not included in their plans. I had to move back in with my mom. I was so lost and broken that I didn't know what to do with myself. My life was flipped upside down, once again. At that time, I met someone who introduced me to marijuana and it helped take the edge off of what I was feeling. It gave me a moment of relief from my agony. I started to smoke frequently and eventually found myself in a relationship with someone who my mom did not approve of. I fell hard; he was my first true love. In desperation, my mom sent me away to live with my aunt once again. Unbeknownst to her, this would get me out of one bad situation and put me into another. The sexual abuse from my uncle picked up right where it left off.

In early spring of my sophomore year, my sister was hit by a car and killed. She was racing with my brother to check the mail and ran across the street without looking. I wanted to be angry with the driver and blame him for what happened, but I eventually learned that he couldn't even function because of what happened. She was only nine years old.

I spent a lot of time being the strong one for my mom and stepdad. Deep in my heart, I felt as though she was the lucky one because she knew Jesus and got to be with Him instead of facing the pain and heartache of this life. I felt like she was saved. Saved from this cruel place called Earth. I eventually moved back with my mom because I felt as though we needed to be close now that my sister was gone. I also wanted to escape the sexual abuse of my uncle.

By the time I entered my junior year of high school, I was completely depleted of any sense of who I was or where I was going in life. I always did well in school but I didn't particularly like it. I had a hard time fitting in socially. I made some friends down the road but they were the wrong kind of friends. They introduced me to methamphetamines. At first, I did it only occasionally. I preferred marijuana and alcohol. I was already high strung so I didn't really need a pick me up. However, I quickly learned that this drug took away all the pain in my life rather than just making me numb. By my senior year, I was heavily involved with meth. I was skipping quite a few of my classes, even though I had a light load.

One day I finally grew sick and tired of the type of people that meth brought into my life. People who would do whatever it took to get their next high, including steal from their close family or me. I had enough and I knew I was better than this life I was living. By the grace of God, I escaped.

My only option to get away from the environment was to move in with my aunt again. The tradeoff was big because I knew that meant the sexual abuse would begin again. I had a tough decision to make but the answer was clear: I had to get off meth, so I returned to my aunt's house. I was able to make it through high school and I walked with my graduating class. It was a proud moment for me as neither of my parents graduated high school. After graduation, I enlisted in the military so I could get the GI Bill and go to college. While partying and living it up before I shipped out to boot camp, I met a man. He was dark skinned and blue eyed. His haunting eyes hooked me. We began what I thought was a fling before I left.

Two weeks before my ship-out date, I found out I was pregnant. My heart sank. I considered my options and decided the next hurdle would be to tell my boyfriend. He handled it well and said he was committed. Again, my mom was very supportive and said that if I wanted to remain in the military, she would watch my baby while I completed boot camp. I knew in my heart that I could never leave another child of mine, even for a short time. I was discharged from the military and had great hopes of building a wonderful future for my child. The father decided he wanted to be a part of the process, but I failed to realize that this man carried giant insecurities that would eventually cause him to become controlling and abusive.

I was only about four months along when our first huge issue came up. My boyfriend started treating me very badly and I couldn't understand why. He was withdrawn and acted like he didn't even want to be with me. He was very angry and I couldn't understand what I had done to make him this way. Little did I know I would spend a lot of time in the future trying to placate his anger. He eventually confessed that he had been unfaithful to me. My heart was broken but I was determined that my child would have the father I never had, no matter the cost. I was once again willing to sacrifice myself for the greater good of my child. He pledged to never hurt me this way again and I blindly believed him. I decided to move in with him at his aunt's house. I thought this would bring us closer together.

The birth of our son was so starkly different from the birth of my first son. I had a sense of joy and excitement instead of dread and emptiness. My labor and delivery were very short. My sweet baby boy came into my world and gave me hope and a purpose. He was the light of my life and I vowed to love him and nurture him in ways I had not been loved and nurtured. At the time, I did not realize what a difficult task that would be. I did not fully understand all of the challenges and heartaches that lay ahead, which would work against my innate desire to give my child all of the things I didn't have.

Soon after our son's birth, my boyfriend started to isolate me from others. He wouldn't allow me to go out on my own and he took our only car to go places by himself, leaving me stranded at home. He eventually became emotionally abusive, calling me names like, "no good, worthless, and crazy." I already had very low self-esteem and this behavior only served to reinforce my negative self-image. I didn't feel worthy of anyone's love. Essentially, he put me in a position where I felt grateful that he would even give me the time of day. It was a dark and twisted time. I felt some of the same hopeless emotions as I did when I gave my first son up for adoption and when I was sexually abused by my uncle. There were times I felt I would fall to pieces emotionally.

> I realized that the very reason I was staying was the very reason I had to leave.

I started to self-medicate again heavily with drugs and alcohol. I desperately needed relief from this pain that threatened to swallow me. We got our own place and things only got worse. My boyfriend began to physically abuse me when he didn't like what I had to say. At one point, he was so out of control, he threw our furniture out the sliding glass door. I was scared enough to finally call the police and he was arrested. Because of all the chaos, we were evicted from our apartment.

We moved back in with his aunt and mom. Once he was out of jail, things were better for a little while but they didn't stay that way. I always thought I would stay with him no matter what. I wanted us to get married and make our son legitimate and I hoped and dreamed of that day. I desperately wanted my son to have his dad in his life, at all costs. I didn't realize the cost would soon become too great. One day I was called into work and my boyfriend got really angry. I think he thought I was cheating on him, out of his own guilty conscience for what he'd done to me. He pinned me on the bed, spat on me, and yelled in my face. He held me captive for over an hour. I will never forget the moment I looked over and my son was watching and crying. It was then that I realized that the very reason I was staying was the very reason I had to leave. I could not have my sweet boy growing up thinking that this is how men treat women. I had to remove him from the chaos if he were ever to have *a chance.*

I moved back to my mom's until I was able to save some money and get on my feet. I got my own place after about six months. I would like to say it was a relief that I was away from my son's father, but my heart ached deeply for all I had lost. I was grieving the loss of my son not having his father, and the loss of love, or the love I thought I had. I didn't know what real love was at that time. Again, I went into a deep depression. As I reflect, I feel sad about all of the things back then that took me away from being the mom I so desired to be. My trauma and the stress of life consumed me and rendered me incapable of being emotionally available for my son. I still spend every day of my life trying to make up for those times.

From there, I drifted into a time in my life where I was angry. Angry with God for all I'd lost and all that had been taken from me. Angry at life for the hand I'd been dealt. Angry with people for the way they disregarded me as a person. I continued to abuse drugs and alcohol as a mechanism to cope with all of the emotions I wanted to bury and hide. I also began an odyssey of sexual addiction. I so desperately needed the attention and love of a man that I was willing to give myself to get it. I realized I was actually pretty and could garner the attention of almost any man I wanted. This became a frequent, dangerous obsession. I went to a club, set my sights on a target, and then conquered. It gave me a feeling of power and control. Unfortunately, the next day left me feeling empty and alone. This cycle continued for a couple of years.

Even though this destructive behavior was going on, I was still attending college and about to graduate with my two-year degree. I knew I needed to make choices about my future and my mind started to go places I didn't expect. I think it was the uncertainty I felt and the perceived need to have someone other than myself to depend on for what was next. I wasn't able to pull my life together on my own, despite my best efforts through self-medication. I also looked at my son and thought, *He needs to know who God is and choose for himself if he wants to believe.* This created a dilemma in my heart because I remembered back to when I was sent to church on the bus and how it crushed me not having my mom with me. I refused to do that to my son, so I decided that I had to go to church too.

I soon began the journey of truly getting to know Christ and learning what it meant to be His follower. He is so gentle and so kind, leading with such grace and truth. The road has not been an easy one; it certainly has not been any storybook ending. It has been very painful because God has lovingly asked me to deal with my pain and trauma through circumstances, relationships, group work, and counseling. I have journeyed down the path that Christ called me to and as I have walked each step, He has traded me beauty for ashes and strength for fear. I can't say that I no longer struggle but the struggle is different. I know that I have Him and He is my "I Am," when I am not. He fills the gap for me when I can't stand and He encourages me to be all that He created me to be. He gave me a *chance* to live, truly live. And now He is giving me the opportunity to pour into others who have walked or are walking similar journeys.

> I have journeyed down the path that Christ called me to and as I have walked each step, He has traded me beauty for ashes and strength for fear.

One of the great things about God is that He uses the things the enemy means for evil, and turns them into something good. Now that I have found a measure of healing, I understand I will never be fully healed this side of heaven. I will always have moments when I feel the shame of who I thought the sexual abuse made me, which was an adulterer. Or the many times I feel I don't measure up because I'm not good enough. It's in those moments that God reminds me of His great grace, His redeeming love. The reason that He came, to heal and restore. He wants to be my all in all. When I am weak, then He is strong. He is showing me that His love covers all and when I feel like I am not enough, He is. I have learned to look to Him for the comfort and encouragement I need. He has also placed wonderful, supportive women around me with whom I can share my pain and receive love and support.

God has called me to minister to other women who are broken and hurting. To be their encouragement when there seems to be none. To show them the same grace and love that God has shown me. He says that we can comfort others with the comfort He has given us in our suffering. The ability to share the burdens of others and to know the pain they are enduring is a blessing I would have never known without the pain I myself endured. It's now my turn to give other women *a chance*. *A chance* to see that they have a choice, *a chance* to see that they matter, *a chance* to love and be loved, *a chance* to make a difference, and *a chance* to fulfill their God-given purpose, their destiny, which God created them for and only they can fulfill. My life's purpose is that they might know Him, that I might fulfill the purpose for which I was sent and share with others the things He has imparted to me. You too deserve *a chance*.

And we know that in all things God works for the good of those who love him, who have been called according to his purpose.
                                                —Romans 8:28 (NIV)

BROKEN

I WAS SEVENTEEN and *broken*.

It was September of my senior year in high school. I was playing varsity volleyball, and for the first time in five years, life seemed to be relatively normal. What happened prior to this point was where the brokenness began.

My biological father and mother were not together when I was born and as a little girl, I lived with my mom and my stepdad, who married when I was four years old. Although I went to visit my biological father on occasion, it was not consistent. My stepfather was an amazing dad and never treated me like anything less than his own. He was patient, kind, loving, and I adored him. He taught me so much about love and consistent parenting that I still value those lessons to this day as a parent myself. Unfortunately, he was not as great a husband, and my parents divorced when I was nine years old.

Together, my mom and stepfather had a little girl. After their divorce, my sister and I would visit our dad regularly, and I would still visit my biological father about once a month. As it is for any child, I remember this being a difficult transition and I was really angry at my mom. I needed someone to blame all my anger on so I took it out on her. I thought she was the reason our family was *broken*.

I had to move school districts in the middle of the year, leave old friends and make new ones, and try to search for my identity. At the time, I didn't realize how insecure and lost I was, but as I look back over my life, I see how this is an area I have struggled with throughout the years. *Broken* marriages, *broken* friendships, a lost, insecure little girl, left feeling alone and *broken*.

When I was eleven, my mom started to date the man who would become my new stepdad. From the very beginning, he was controlling and came into our lives determined to change what we considered our new normal. He had an issue with the visitation I had with my first stepfather and said I needed to have regular visits with my biological father instead, regardless of what I wanted or what was best for my sister and me. Over the years, I had maintained a relationship with my biological father that was limited and inconsistent, so stopping all visits with the man I called my dad just made me dislike my mom's boyfriend even more. As I spent more time with my biological father and family, I developed a stronger bond with them.

Despite the fighting and difficult times we had during the months my mom dated this man, they decided to get married, and we became a blended family when I was twelve. Life at home changed once again and now there was another sibling on the way.

So at the ripe old age of twelve, I had moved homes seven different times, attended three different elementary schools, and was currently attending middle school. The next year we moved again and I started yet another new school. Once more, I can look back and see how insecure I was. Not able to establish lasting friendships, a home life that was unstable with fighting and abuse, and a lot of built up anger made me confused about who I really was. I considered myself a chameleon. I could change my personality to fit in with who I needed to be in order make friends. As my relationship grew with my father, stepmother, and siblings, I asked my mother if I could move away, but she would not consider it. I had moved so many times it didn't make much of a difference to me and I thought that I could find stability and be happy. I wasn't allowed to, so life at home continued to spiral down a dark path.

When I was fourteen, life started to change once again, but not for the better. Now in high school, home became increasingly abusive and the fighting escalated. My stepfather became more verbally abusive with my sister and me, but when it came to the physical abuse, I fought back so most of that landed on my little sister. I would often overhear my mom and stepdad fighting, and my mom complained he was hurting her and she'd beg him to stop. My hatred for him increased and I wanted to be anywhere but home.

I never understood how my mom could stay with him. It felt as though she chose him over my sister and me. He was hurting us and life at home was anything but good. What I wanted was to have a family I could love, and one who would love me in return. This began my downward spiral toward making bad choices and becoming rebellious.

At fifteen, I was introduced to a guy who soon became my boyfriend. He liked me and was extremely kind in the beginning. I thought I had finally found someone who cared about me, loved me, and made me happy. Like a lot of teenagers, we made bad choices and started drinking and partying.

There was a time I went to my mother to talk about some inappropriate behaviors of my current stepfather and I was able to tell her what was happening and how I felt. We sat in a high school parking lot after one of my practices and I explained that my stepfather had been making me feel uncomfortable with touching and physical attention. She went home and addressed the situation with him but he instantly denied it and said I was lying to get attention. I didn't go home that night but when I did, I felt devastated and betrayed that my mother took his side.

After some time went by, I shared my frustration and pain with a friend of mine. She immediately told me I needed to talk to the school counselor to try and get through this. The day I went to my school counselor, Child Protective Services came in and prevented me from going home. It wasn't exactly how I imagined it would happen. I thought I would just be able to find ways to make home life better and get advice. Since I couldn't go home, I stayed with a friend for almost two weeks before my mom called to tell me that I would be moving

> What I wanted was to have a family I could love, and one who would love me in return.

to live with my biological father. Although I had been visiting my dad regularly since the age of twelve and had a great relationship with my family, it wasn't an easy transition moving to another city.

The reason for my biological parents splitting before I was born was because my dad was in another relationship at the time he was dating my mother. When my mother found out she was pregnant, the other woman found out she was pregnant too. My dad married his other girlfriend and together they had four children. I was moving to a new town, to another new school, away from all of my friends, and I was about to try and fit in with a sister who was thirteen days older than I was. Visiting was one thing, but sharing friends and lives was a whole new ball game. It seemed as though every relationship I had in my life was completely *broken*.

The next six months were a little hazy. I fell into a deep depression. I saw a psychiatrist who came to school every week, and the truth is I was suicidal. I ran away three times and got caught every time. Life at my dad's was actually the healthiest home I had lived in in a long time but I was fifteen and my friends were an important part of my life. They were my stability and confidants during the difficult times in my life. I was willing to do anything to get back to my old life, including telling CPS I had exaggerated the abuse and it didn't happen the way I said it did.

My mom promised that things had changed at home and life would be better. Charges were dropped and once I finished my sophomore year, I moved back to my mom's house. Although my stepfather apologized for making me out to be a liar, he promised things would be different this time around. Unfortunately, this promise only lasted a couple of months and I once again found myself moving into another home. I stayed with my childhood best friend's family temporarily and then moved in with my first stepdad and his family.

During my junior year of high school, I loved life. I was back with my friends, and school seemed to be going well. I wasn't deal-ing with fighting at home but I was not making good choices as I continued to party and hid it very well. My boyfriend and I were on and off again and it was not a healthy relationship, but I thought I could make it work. I was a *broken* girl, paired with a *broken* boy, trying to force something good to come out of our brokenness.

My mom convinced me to move back in with her for my senior year, again promising that it would all be different this time around, so I tried to move home once again.

All seemed to be going well at home for the first time in years. I was enjoying my senior year, playing varsity volleyball and enjoying my friends. My relationship with my mom was better than it had been in a long time and I thought this year might just be what I had been waiting for. I was desperate for a healthy relationship and was hungry for love.

I came home from school one day in early October and knew something was not right. I was not feeling well and had been more tired than usual. I didn't think it was possible, but I went to the store to pick up a pregnancy test just to be certain. The test showed two pink lines indicating I was pregnant…I was in complete shock! I was sitting there in disbelief as I called my best friend to tell her. She immediately came over and we went straight to the store to buy another test to be sure the first one was not a false positive. Just like the first one, the second test came out positive and we both sat and cried. I knew my life was going to change, but I had no idea to the extent that it would.

I called my boyfriend and asked him to meet me so we could talk. After I told him the news, he gave me an ultimatum to have an abortion or he would not stay with me. I was devastated, but not shocked that this was his reaction. I refused and told him that if he chose not to be a dad, I wouldn't ask him to, but that I would not abort the baby. Leading to yet another *broken* relationship and ultimately a *broken* heart.

Two weeks later, my mom confronted me and I broke down with all of the emotions I had built up. She reassured me that it was all going to be okay but I could see in her eyes the devastation and hurt she felt. She knew all too well what it was like to be a single mom and no matter how much she helped and gave her support, my life now was going to shift and the road would become even more difficult.

After telling my mom, my ex-boyfriend became extremely angry. For the first time abortion crossed my mind as a possible solution. I began to feel pressure and second-guess my decision. Not only was my ex-boyfriend unkind, but teachers, other parents, and my peers were talking about me. My self-esteem was shot and I wanted all of this craziness to go away.

After a long conversation, my mom assured me that although this was not going to be an easy time in my life, she would be there to help me along the way and it was going to be all right. To this day, I am so glad that I chose my son over the temporary pain and discomfort of what others thought of me. He is the best decision I ever made!

Over the next nine months of my pregnancy, my relationship with my ex continued to spiral downward and we fought constantly. I kept thinking that if only I could make it work, we could be a family and I could prove all those doubters wrong. I wanted a two-parent home for my son and I was willing to put up with whatever I needed to in order to provide that for him. What I didn't realize at the time was that I was providing the same unhealthy home life I had fought so hard to get away from. Still, I thought he would change and once our little boy came, he would want to be with us and be a family.

After my son was born, I discovered a love I never knew existed. My son was the most perfect little human and I was infatuated with this perfect gift. At this point, I was willing to try and make things work with his dad and soon moved in with his parents. After six months of trying to force a relationship that was never stable in the first place, I moved out on my own for the first time at the age of nineteen. After attending college for a year right out of high school, I found that I was not prepared for the busy life of being a mom, going to school, and working. I stopped pursuing my education and started a job as a bank teller. I was trying to create something "normal" and gain some stability.

> I am so glad that I chose my son over the temporary pain and discomfort of what others thought of me.

I began dating a wonderful man. He came from a great family and seemed to have so much going for himself. When we began talking, I didn't think it would ever become anything serious because after all, I was a single mom without support from family. He was recovering from an accident that nearly took his life, so he wasn't able to go away to college. He planned to move away the following summer.

That summer, my boyfriend went away to college at Washington State University, in Pullman, Washington. The next four years were challenging and it was difficult to continue a long-distance relationship, but what we had was different from anything I had ever experienced before.

He was kind, thoughtful, committed, he believed in me, and most importantly, he was good to my son. Not only did I think I would never find someone who would want to date me because I was a single mom, but I also didn't think I deserved anyone who was so good to me. We had struggled while dating and definitely did not have the "perfect" relationship, but we struggled in a healthy and committed way. Long gone were the days of verbal abuse such as I had experienced in past relationships. Instead, we learned how to disagree and compromise while respecting one another.

In the fall, I was accepted to Washington State University and moved to Pullman. However, I was court ordered to move back home after a battle with my son's father. He argued that I could attend school closer to home so I moved back and continued a long distance relationship with my boyfriend while he was away at college. There were many miles traveled between us and it was a struggle to make it work.

After five years of dating, we married and then and only then, lived together because we wanted to wait until we said, "I do." Although I was excited to be married and I loved my new life as a family of three, I still struggled with feelings of abandonment because of my childhood experiences. I consistently tried to find acceptance from others. I was insecure with who I was as a person and wondered if I was good enough to be loved forever, or if my husband would leave me for someone better. I hadn't really internalized what I was feeling nor did I take the time to figure it all out until much later in my marriage. I hid those feelings deep inside and put on a strong and resilient face for the rest of the world to see. I went back to school to finish what I started. Even after all of this time and after everything I had accomplished, I still had people who doubted me and told me I would never finish school. Still, in my late twenties, I had family members, whom I loved dearly, putting me down and making me feel like I would never succeed. With their "good intentions" of "trying to motivate me" toward getting my degree, all it did was create more doubt in my mind about who I was, and what I was worth. Still, I kept fighting and was desperate to prove that I was worthy.

With the support of my new husband, I attended Yakima Valley Community College where I received my AA degree. After the devastation of not being able to attend WSU when I was forced to move home, I attended WSU online and graduated with my Bachelor of Science degree. I finally fulfilled my dream of being a Cougar! Yet there was still a piece missing and I just couldn't quite figure out what it was.

A few years went by and one day my mother and I had a serious talk about when I was a girl. My mother finally left my stepfather and she told me that my ex-stepfather confessed everything, including details I was unaware of. Apparently, he gave me sleeping pills and I was sexually molested without even being aware of it. You may not understand, but it was so freeing for me. So many times, I had been told I was just a bratty child trying to cause problems at home that I really began to believe I was crazy. For the first time ever, my mother said she believed me and she was sorry. A huge weight was lifted from my shoulders!

I was finally able to confront my ex-stepfather about the abuse from my childhood. After all the years of the shame, being called a liar and being hated by so many who swore I was making it all up, I was able to lay it all to rest. This was a difficult chapter in my life, but it gave me so much healing and closure. Still, I was not who I wanted to be and I couldn't understand what was missing.

It wasn't until I agreed to attend my sister's church that I found the missing piece. My sister regularly invited our family to join her family. She never pushed me or made me feel bad for turning her down, but she never gave up believing that this was going to be life changing for all of us. After my first time visiting Memorial Bible Church (MBC), I found a love I had never known before. I was a Christian and believed in Jesus Christ, but I had never really known or followed Him. I realized my beliefs about Christianity and my relationship with Christ had not even scratched the surface.

My family continued to attend MBC over the years and we have developed a love and respect for God unlike anything I ever imagined. The void in my life that I searched for all of those years was now overflowing with the grace, love, and mercy of God. So many times, I wondered who was I to be loved unconditionally when I had made so many mistakes in my life. But what I finally realized was that it was the amazing grace of God, the love He poured out for me, and the forgiveness of all my wrongdoings that set me free. Free to be okay with my mistakes, free to love myself for who I was, and free to be better today than I was yesterday. The biggest thing holding me back was myself.

I am where I am because I didn't give up and I didn't give in to what others around me said.

Jesus laid down His life for mine, yours, and everyone else in this world so that we can be forgiven and be free. The problem was I thought I was going to be the one to fix it all. Pretty arrogant, right? I mean, who honestly thinks we can do it better than Jesus can? Who can take away our worries, carry our burdens, and make us whole again? Who can turn our sorrow, strife, and brokenness into something undeniably and unbelievably beautiful? The one and only, King of Kings can, not me! That is one of the reasons I love the verse in Proverbs 3:5: *Trust in the Lord with all your heart and lean not on your own understanding; in all your ways submit to him, and he will make your paths straight.* For so many years, I put "me" in place of "he" in this verse. For so long I depended on my own understanding and tried to make things work on my own. I did it the world's way rather than God's way. The weight of the world was lifted from my shoulders as I learned to allow Jesus to guide me.

Today, my husband and I have been together for sixteen years. We have been married for eleven, and have three beautiful children. He adopted my oldest son who is seventeen, and together we had our daughter who is nine and youngest son who is seven. A few years after I finished my bachelor's degree from Washington State University, I continued with school to finish my master's in education. I am now teaching fifth grade language arts and love it. We attend and serve at Christ the King Community Church where I lead worship on Sundays and my oldest son helps with production. We absolutely love our church family!

I am where I am because I didn't give up and I didn't give in to what others around me said. I refused to become a statistic and I refused to allow my son to become one as well. I held on to my belief that if you don't like something, you can make a choice to change it.

I was a lost little girl, surrounded by *broken* relationships, trying to put them back together and seeking others to make me feel whole and complete. In my brokenness, I realized that only one person could make me feel the way I was desperately searching for. It was in my weakest moments I had to learn to look up to a perfect God instead of out to a world of other *broken* people, including myself. I learned that God has the ability to strengthen us in our weakness, give us beauty for our ashes, heal our hurts, and make something far better out of what we see as *broken*.

The LORD is close to the brokenhearted and saves those who are crushed in spirit.

—Psalm 34:18 (NIV)

PICKING UP THE PIECES

BORN IN EARLY June at Valley General Hospital in Seattle, Washington, I entered this world as a textbook Gemini. My entire life, I have exhibited all the classic Gemini traits. I am creative, versatile, witty, and intellectual. To balance that out, I am also unfocused, anxious, dramatic, and most of all, strong-willed. I was a happy baby, when I wasn't a mad baby. I was a cheerful child, when I wasn't an angry child. I was a pleasant teen, when I got my way.

Needless to say, I presented many challenges to my parents as I grew up in contrast to my completely agreeable, complacent older sister. I didn't make life easy for them. I suppose it's why early on in my childhood, as early as I can remember, my parents decided that giving in to me was just easier than fighting with me. I grew up surrounded by a great deal of love and with wonderful examples of kindness and positive moral behavior that I'm so thankful for because it forged my character at my core. However, without much discipline, and with unmerited trust, I learned quickly that I called the shots in my life and as I entered my teen years, I used this to my full advantage as often as possible.

My elementary school years were fairly uneventful and "normal" aside from my lack of energy and desire to play or engage in sports as my peers did. I often felt as though I had the flu when I woke in the morning and I don't remember going a day without a headache. Without any other symptoms, I was always told that nothing was wrong with me and developed a reputation among my family and friends as being a hypochondriac.

Knowing that I truly felt terrible but receiving very little validation, my self-confidence began to plummet and by my junior high years, I was clinically depressed. I have often said that there isn't enough money in the world to pay me to go back to junior high. It was a miserable time for me and though I had many friends and appeared to have a positive social life, including consistent involvement in my church youth group, I felt that I was alone in a black hole I would never be able to get out of. Suicide was always on my mind, which made me even more depressed because I knew it was a sin and that I was not honoring God with those thoughts.

Somehow, I made it through those years and started coming out of my depression as I entered my freshman year of high school. Around the same time, I started to examine my life and the people in it quite carefully and concluded that my friendships were insincere. Over the course of my freshman year, I pulled further away from the clique of popular kids I had always hung around with and gravitated more toward the "skaters," who I found to be much more accepting of people. These were the kids I spent the majority of my time with during high school, though I still remained in contact with my old friends to some degree.

By my junior year, I began to realize it wasn't the people I was hanging out with who were the problem, it was me. I just wasn't happy and felt bored with my life. I still struggled greatly with always feeling sick but became used to that black cloud hovering over me and accepted it as me being "crazy." Ten years later, I was diagnosed with childhood-onset fibromyalgia. The validation of the diagnosis alone was in itself the most effective treatment I received for the depression. However, I was still a teenager and restless. My life became about searching for something better.

When my mom was offered a job out of state, I was ecstatic! I knew that was the change I needed. After living in Maple Valley, Washington, all seventeen years of my life, my mom and I packed up the car and moved south to beautiful Bend, Oregon, a place where we had vacationed during the summer a number of times. By this time, my sister had already graduated from high school so she planned to stay in the Seattle area where she was working and attending school. My dad joined us in Bend nearly a year later once our house sold and he secured a job in Central Oregon. Though I had no idea what to expect by starting life over as a senior in high school, I was willing and excited to make this much needed change in my repetitive and seemingly unsatisfying life. As a mature, straight-A student who was active in the church and had her sights set on medical school, what could possibly go wrong?

Soon after the move, I nailed down an after-school job at a local video store where I met my first friend in this new town. She was one year ahead of me in school and had already graduated. She had a large network of friends, both older and younger, to whom she introduced me. Before school even started, I was well on my way to having an exciting social life.

Although I was mature for my age, smart, and a churchgoing girl, I was also a teenager and therefore, wasn't against enjoying a weekend party with my new friends. It was at one of these parties I met a man who was five years older than I was. He was handsome and charming. With his brand new, shiny white truck and captivating blue eyes, it wasn't long before I had a major crush on him. Only a few days after first meeting him, I found out he and his roommate were evicted from their apartment and left with nowhere to live. Without hesitation I begged my mother to let these, "really nice guys who were just down on their luck," crash with us until they could figure something else out. She said, "Yes." We couldn't possibly have imagined the life-altering turn of events this would lead to. A lifetime of *picking up the pieces*.

With an intense infatuation at the core of my thought process, it wasn't hard for this man I was crushing on to come up with all the right things to say. It led to intimacy quickly. I was very conflicted between my intense feelings for him and my desire to take things slower than he wanted. Even though I made this clear to him, hesitated, and protested, I eventually surrendered to his charm.

A late period and some serious nausea had me at the doorstep of the Birthright of Bend clinic where my pregnancy was confirmed. One of my close girlfriends went with me and afterward we just sat in a booth at a nearby Taco Bell as I stared blankly into space with no clue of how

I felt alone, my heart broken into little pieces, scattered everywhere.

to proceed. It was a Friday, and he had gone out of town for the weekend, so I spent the weekend nervously awaiting his return. I had no idea how I was going to tell this man that I was carrying his child. I imagined something much different from what turned out to be the reality. When he returned, I asked him to sit down and told him I needed to tell him something that was really hard for me to say. He was calm and encouraged me to just tell him what was on my mind. When I was finally able to mutter the words "I'm pregnant," he looked at me, still calm, and thoughtfully said, "Well, I'll pay for it." At first it was unclear to me what he meant by this. But observing the way he still appeared so calm and disconnected, I realized he meant he would pay for an abortion. This definitely was not the romanticized scenario that had played out in my head! I told him there was no chance I would have an abortion. With that, he packed his belongings and moved out of my house, and out of my life. Up until that time, and not again since, have I wept with as much despair and hopelessness as I did on that day. I felt alone, my heart broken into little pieces, scattered everywhere. It was then I knew he would not be there to help with *picking up the pieces.*

I knew I was going to need my mom more than ever. That night, I faced her and broke the news. As expected, she cried for the struggles she knew I would face but she also embraced me and assured me that I was never going to be alone and that my baby was going to be loved to the moon and back.

Together, we called my dad, who was still living in Washington at that point, and told him over the phone. His reaction was not quite as tender as my mom's was. Without giving me any kind of response, he hung up the phone. We didn't speak again until six months later.

From the day I was born, my daddy took his job as my protector and my hero very seriously. I never doubted that he would catch me if I fell or that he would help me find a way to make things right if there was a need. Though it hurt me terribly that my dad wouldn't speak to me and couldn't even look me in the eye, I also knew that his reaction came from a place of total despair for the loss of my childhood as well as from his own sense of guilt for not having been there to prevent my pregnancy from happening.

It was knowing this, combined with my total belief in his love for me, which kept me from losing hope that our relationship would heal.

The first trimester was a nightmare as I was plagued with the worst possible case of morning sickness. I lost fourteen pounds overnight from severe vomiting and spent a great deal of my time admitted to the hospital, battling dehydration. I was seventeen, pregnant, a sickly skeleton of my former self, and in a black hole of depression that seemed to have no escape!

What kept me going was the love I already felt for my child, the love I knew God placed in my heart, which was just a smidgen of His love for me. When I wasn't hovering over a toilet bowl or hooked up to an IV at the hospital, I was buckling down at school and desperately trying to continue to work. My employers at the video store kept me on as long as they could but finally suggested that I resign. It was the best thing for me, really. I put all of my energy into finishing school and planning a life for my baby and me. Having more than enough credits, I was able to graduate from high school at the mid-term semester. Though I didn't finish with a 4.0 cumulative as I had always intended, I was able to finish with a respectable 3.7 GPA.

With my school days behind me, and still five months until my due date, I found a new job at a coffee stand. Still pretty sick, the smell of coffee was hard on me and as my pregnancy progressed, so was standing all day. The job, however, was such a blessing and allowed me to save a great deal of money for my baby's upcoming arrival.

When I was twenty weeks along, I found out that I was having a girl. At this point, my dad and I still hadn't had a face-to-face conversation. When my mom called to tell him the baby's sex, the joy I heard in his voice when he said, "Ohhhhh! A baby girl," was enough for me to know that my daddy was on my side and would remain my knight in shining armor.

By my last two months of pregnancy, I was finally over being sick and had successfully gained back all of the weight I lost, plus thirty pounds more.

On my actual due date, after thirty-six hours of natural labor, I delivered my precious girl. The moment I laid eyes on her, I experienced a joy that cannot be described in words and a love that surpassed anything I thought I could feel. My baby girl was my angel sent from above to put me on the path of life for which I knew I was meant.

Since her dad was so much older than I was and given the fact that he was unwilling to accept any responsibility for my pregnancy, my parents were advised early in my pregnancy to use the legal system to handle those issues. After appearing in court, her dad admitted that he was responsible for my pregnancy and the judge ordered him to sign the birth certificate when the baby arrived. So when my baby was just one day old and we were still at the hospital, he arrived to sign the birth certificate. He was invited into my family birthing room where he excitedly accepted my offer to hold his daughter. I was in awe as I watched him confidently hold her in his arms and look at her with complete adoration and amazement. He spoke to her very briefly and told her that he loved her. Then, despite the spark of hope that was ignited in me, he walked out of my life, and his daughter's life, yet again. Thankfully, my parents were there, *picking up the pieces*.

For the first six months of my daughter's life, I continued living with my mom. During this time our home in Washington finally sold, and my dad was able to join us in Bend. We were very excited to have him finally home!

Life as a single teenage mom was a challenge I took on with great determination. I had an expectation of myself to do this "job" better than any mom out there would, regardless of age. I made it known that my baby would be the cleanest, best-dressed, most-disciplined, well-educated, and respectful child in town! I vowed that I absolutely would not behave like, nor be seen as, the stereotypical teen parent. Knowing that I would not be able to spend a moment away from my baby, and that no one else could care for her as I could, I moved into my own apartment and began a career in childcare. This became a very reputable and profitable home business for me. This choice made it possible for my daughter to spend her early childhood years at home with me.

I met my husband-to-be when my daughter was one. The sound of the waste disposal truck woke me from my sleep so I jumped out of bed and chased the truck down the road, in the rain, barefoot, long hair in tangles and wearing my favorite men's flannel pajamas from Goodwill. I'd forgotten to put the garbage out! I was quite a sight, no doubt. The young, handsome driver of the truck was more than willing to go back and empty my cans. I learned later that he drove back by my house multiple times that day looking for me. Just a few weeks later, my best friend and roommate had a Christmas party at work so she asked an old friend she ran into if he would be her date. After the party, he drove her home and realized that her house was also my house. For the next few weeks, he showed up at the house when he got off work around 2:00 p.m. to "wait for my roommate to get home from work" which was typically around 6:00 p.m. By all appearances, it was my roommate and this cute garbage truck driver who had started a relationship, but it didn't take long for my very perceptive friend to recognize the chemistry between him and me, so she gracefully acknowledged that and gave us her full blessing to be together. My daughter had just turned one and he courageously took on the role of father and has been "Dad" ever since.

He grew up in a very large family with his mother being one of the oldest of thirteen children. With most of his aunts and uncles living in the area, he was surrounded by cousins of all ages for the entire duration of his childhood and adolescence, which allowed him to step right into the role of "parent" without even blinking. There is no denying that he was uncomfortable with little things here and there, like my daughter wanting to sleep in the bed with us, for example, but in the big picture, he met the challenge of his new role with great maturity and acceptance.

This kindhearted, loving man eventually asked me to marry him, and without hesitation I said "Yes!" My daughter was a month away from her third birthday.

When my little girl was four years old, her biological father contacted me and asked if he could meet her. I agreed without hesitation. I always said that I would give him one chance, and one chance only. We all met at a park on a Sunday afternoon where father and daughter had a fine time visiting and playing. It was nerve-racking and exciting but scary and confusing for me. But overall, my heart was joyous for her to have this opportunity. After the visit, we planned to meet again the following Sunday. He didn't show up. A few weeks later, he called and apologized profusely with an excuse about being stuck out of town. That was the moment my resolve to follow through with my own convictions took over. I told him that he would not play with my daughter's heart by coming in and out of her life as he pleased and that his one chance had come and gone. He was not to contact us again, and he didn't.

For the majority of her young life, her biological father lived with his wife and their twin sons within a few miles of us, but was completely and totally absent from our life, physically, emotionally, and financially. Even though a support order was in place, he never worked a job consistently enough that would allow for any garnishment so I never received any child support from him.

When my little girl was twelve, she desperately wanted to make contact with her biological father again, so we did. He acted very grateful and said he had been hoping and praying for that day to come and only stayed away because I told him to. With only her interests in mind, I agreed to let her spend some time with him again. Their time together was full of laughter, stories, pillow fights, and heartfelt conversation. It lasted one day. She did not hear from him again. This time she said, "Never again." My husband and I were there for her, *picking up the pieces.*

But at seventeen, she did contact him again through Facebook. He had moved from Oregon to Texas the year prior so was no longer close enough for a physical visit. Somehow, they actually began developing a relationship through phone contact and messaging that blessedly provided her with a much-needed piece of her life puzzle. This was a key time in my life as well because her biological father and I had the first real conversations we ever had. Not only did I receive apologies from him that I felt were completely genuine, but more importantly, I was able to forgive him. He told me that I should hate him. My answer was honest and easier to come by than you might imagine. How could I hate someone who was a part of creating my beautiful child? I told him that to wish any of what happened away would be to wish away not only my daughter, but also the family I have now, and that would be unimaginable. And with that, I thanked him, because without having had him in my life, my life would not be what it is now. We were on the phone for this conversation, but it was clear that he was sobbing. He thanked me from the bottom of his heart for saying all of that to him. When I hung up the phone, I cried nearly as intensely as when he first walked away from me. This time though, it was not from a place of sadness. It was from the realization that I had just released myself from the cage I had kept myself in for eighteen years. A cage full of resentment, sadness, confusion, anger, and fear. In that moment, I was no longer a teen mom governed by the stigma of where I went wrong. I was just a mom. I was a mom who loved my daughter and family so much that all I could see was each and

> I nearly ran myself into the ground both physically and emotionally trying to meet the expectations of myself.

every blessing that brought me to them. I no longer had to prove I could do a good job because I knew I already had done a good job.

When my daughter was eighteen, her biological father flew her and her brothers to Texas for a family reunion. She spent time with grandparents, aunts, uncles, and cousins in addition to her biological father and brothers. She had a wonderful time.

Shortly after her return home, she was given the news that her biological father had cancer and was terminal. Six months later, soon after turning nineteen years old, she was grieving his death. Again, my husband and I were there, *picking up the pieces.*

Twenty years and three more kids later, I still struggle with the need to prove that I am able to provide not only just enough but much more than enough for my family. I continued my home daycare business, which allowed me to stay home with all of our sons, and continue to make an incredible income. I've also discovered I carry a fear of "what will people think" around with me when forming the expectations I have for my children's behavior. This mindset is what I now refer to as my "teen-mom complex." In some respects, this mindset was a good thing because it guided me and ensured that I made every possible effort to instill positive character traits in my kids who now at twenty-one, nineteen, sixteen, and fourteen, are all truly spectacular people. On the other hand, I nearly ran myself into the ground both physically and emotionally trying to meet the expectations of myself. I mellowed out some, and found a happy medium in order to avoid damaging the rest of them with my own insecurities. Nonetheless, I have harbored a sense of guilt over the years for being, what I felt, too hard on my little girl. Regretfully, I admit that my eldest carried much too heavy a burden on her shoulders at a very young age because of my high expectations of her. Thankfully, she tells me now that she wouldn't change a thing about how I raised her. With that validation from her, in addition to wisdom gained over the years, I am learning to forgive myself and move on.

While I was working on this story for Starting Point, I was surprised to learn that my now twenty-one-year-old daughter, who recently gave birth to her own son, has also been the subject of a similar book project that a friend of hers is working on through a church group. I have not seen the whole of her interview, but my daughter felt compelled to share with me her response to the following question:

"Do you ever idolize other moms and wish you could be like them? If so, Why?"

Her reply was:

"Yes, I do. I idolize my mother. I have never met another person who has been able to accomplish as much as she has. My mother had me right after she turned eighteen. She started a daycare when I was a baby so that she could get every possible minute with me. She has continued to run her daycare for twenty years in order to be closer to my brothers and me. She cooks, cleans, works her butt off every day, and has learned so many incredible things. From crocheting and sewing blankets, clothes, and many other incredible items, to paying the bills, balancing four children who have sports, and all the other joys that come with raising insane athletes with too many needs, I would say that my mother truly is super woman. She has always done her best to make sure we have everything we need and want, even if she can't afford it. Her whole life revolves around making her family happy. This is why she is my idol. She went from an eighteen-year-old single mother to the most accomplished woman I have ever met and she still continues to blow me away with everything she does now and is doing for her grandson."

Life hasn't been perfect for us, not even close. As a family, we have faced struggles that threatened to tear us apart. We have been in the trenches of addiction and experienced firsthand the horror of all that comes with it. We have betrayed trust. We have said and done things to each other that can't be taken back but thankfully can and have been forgiven. In hindsight, it's clear to see that the majority of our family's turmoil has occurred when we were turned away from God, when our eyes were set on what we thought we knew was best for us instead of being set on Him and trusting that His path for us is already paved. We have truly damaged

> God's plan for all of us is bigger than anything we could ever plan for ourselves

each other at different times, but each time our God has repaired us. We are a family, and more importantly, we are a faithful family. By the grace of God, we have weathered the storms and our family has come out stronger and more convicted in our faith each time. Without the knowledge that God's plan for all of us is bigger than anything we could ever plan for ourselves, and that His love for us is greater than any love we could imagine, I would have been lost, and my family would have been lost, too. Through our faith in God, and because of His promise to us, we are whole and we are still pushing through the storms of life that we know will one day lead to an eternity of sunshine in His presence.

God has always been there. Without Him, we would all still be broken pieces scattered by the storm. He is always faithful and has always been there by my side, *picking up the pieces.*

God, pick up the pieces. Put me back together again.
—Jeremiah 17:14 (MSG)

TAKEN AWAY

AS A LITTLE girl, I was very much a tomboy. I paid no attention to the dirt under my nails or to my uncombed hair. I loved to play outside and climbed trees as high as they would take me. I didn't have a care in the world. My parents told me I was half human and half monkey. My sisters made fun of me for believing them. I learned the meaning of the word *gullible* at an early age—and that I was way too sensitive. The moment I felt like I was being teased, I would run to my room or to my mother.

If I wasn't running away from my sisters, I was chasing after them. As the youngest in my family, I was always tagging along. In the summer, we would catch frogs in the swampy creek or play hide-and-seek in the tall grass near our home. We loved to play in what we called the "dirt hills," a large undeveloped area of land close to our neighborhood.

I spent much of my childhood in those dirt hills. When the older kids weren't around, I would play with the younger children in the neighborhood. We would make forts out of branches and climb to places where no one could boss us around. If we weren't in the trees, we were kicking up dirt from the dusty ground. Many times, I would go home with a dirty face and filthy hands, until one day, I went home feeling dirty on the inside too.

He was seven years old and I was five. He hid the magazines under some branches behind a rock in the trees and told me not to tell anyone. More than once, he wanted to look at the pictures, until we would hear someone coming and he'd hide them again. I felt guilty for looking, and deep down something told me it was wrong. Seeds of guilt and shame were planted in my heart.

I will never forget the time our parents went away for the weekend, and we stayed at our friend's home. The sleeping arrangements consisted of the older children sleeping in one room, and the younger ones in another, which put me in the boy's bedroom. During the night, he asked me to take off all my clothes—just like we saw on the pages of the magazines. And I did. Even though we didn't go any further, I went to sleep that night feeling alone and ashamed. At an early age, my innocence seemed to have been quickly *taken away.*

Our family began attending church when I was in the second grade.

I learned in Sunday school that Jesus took away sins, but mine didn't seem to want to go even when I asked Him to take them.

I was nine when I accepted Jesus into my heart, but I wasn't sure if He accepted me. It wasn't enough to quiet the critical voice in my head; the one that said you're not good enough and you never will be.

When I was ten, my parents decided to have another child. I was excited to be a big sister until the next one came, and the next one, and the next one, and the next one. During the time I was age eleven to sixteen, our family grew from five to ten. I love my large family now, but resentfulness grew with the arrival of each new sibling. I was both embarrassed and defensive of our growing family.

It felt like, with the demands of so many children, my parent's love and attention was *taken away.*

I have fond memories of my childhood. I loved playing sports, helping my mother in her vegetable garden, and spending endless hours in the treehouse my dad built for us girls. My parents were actively involved with my school and extracurricular activities. My mom was my Girl Scout leader and my dad coached my soccer and softball teams. However, as our family grew, it was difficult for them to stay connected. That said, my own insecurities made it feel nearly impossible for me to approach my parents about personal struggles or general questions about life, especially with regard to boy-girl relationships. I wasn't comfortable talking to my parents about anything related to the opposite sex. When I was a preteen, my parents gave me a book to read on my own about intercourse but I was disgusted by what I read, which was typical for that age. I viewed it as a very dirty thing. I think a large part of it had to do with the early exposure I'd had to pornography.

By the time I entered junior high school, I distanced myself from my parents. I grew apart from my long-time friends too, including my best friend, all for the sake of hanging out with the popular crowd. I kept my grades up, but cared more about my social life and continued to crave attention from the boys.

At the age of fifteen, my dad bought me a ring as a symbol to remain pure until marriage and talked with me about dating. By choosing to wear it, I was making a promise to him and to God. I loved the ring but didn't plan on dating anyone, mainly out of fear of my dad's intimidating approach. When my sister brought home a potential date, he was put through the wringer by a series of questions. I didn't want to put any boy through that, especially one I liked.

I was all for saving myself until marriage and had no intention of giving myself away. More than anything, I just wanted to be liked. The first time I was kissed by a boy, I broke up with him the next day.

I began to compromise my values during my freshman year of high school. I spent less time trying to impress my teachers with my work and more time trying to impress the boys. I was drawn to students who would goof off in class or make fun of other students for their ridiculously styled hair, lack of personal hygiene, or generic brand shoes. I spent the last half of the school year hanging out with the not-so-nice kids. I began doing reckless things like smoking cigarettes and stealing things at the mall. Eventually, I got caught, which was enough to put an end to it, but only for a while.

Once the school year came to a close, my mom caught me in a lie. I wasn't where I was supposed to be. My dad found out and came to pick me up. Not only was I in trouble for lying, but my clothes reeked of cigarette smoke. I was grounded for the entire summer. The only places I could go were to church and the mailbox.

It wasn't long before I began sneaking out at night. I would hop into cars with strangers to get to my destination quicker, sometimes with a friend, but many times alone. I am thankful to be alive. Whether it was to watch the drama unfold at the bowling alley or to smoke cigarettes on the members-only golf course, I was in. This gave me feelings of freedom and independence, but my biggest motivation depended on who would be there. Just like many teens, I confused lust with love and being wanted with getting used. The last time I snuck out that summer was when the guys we were hanging out with introduced us girls to drugs. I didn't want anything to do with it. The thought of letting a drug take control of me was enough to scare me out of it. I remember hightailing it home without hitching a ride.

I spent the last week of summer at camp where I gave my life to Jesus, again. I left with my camp counselor's Bible, not because I stole it, but because she gave it to me. She wrote a verse in the front, *I can do all things through Christ who strengthens me* (Philippians 4:13). She continued to reach out to me with encouraging letters and I was determined to change for the better.

It wasn't long after turning sixteen that my parents put our house up for sale. I was not fond of the idea at all. My parents hoped to buy a house out in the country but it fell through so we ended up moving about fifteen minutes away. I may have been able to get a variance for school, but I had already said my good-byes and was depressed. My sister was getting married and I felt lost in the mix.

I ended up homeschooling the rest of that year. The following summer, I started hanging out with my best guy friend from high school. We had been friends since our elementary days. I made it clear to my parents we were just friends—which was true, until he kissed me unexpectedly and I didn't bail on him for it. Soon we were boyfriend and girlfriend. We spent a lot of time together. I was convinced we were made for each other and that someday we would get married.

I confused lust with love and being wanted with getting used.

By the end of the summer, I gave my heart to him as well as my virginity.

I figured it wouldn't matter since most likely we would be together forever...

We were not.

I convinced my parents to let me go back to public school beginning my junior year. They let me, but by January, there would be another move. This time it would be further away. I was devastated. It was tough enough to move from one school to the next, let alone again in the middle of my junior year.

My parents allowed me to live with a friend to finish off the school year, but after a few months my boyfriend and I had ended. I moved back home and ended up meeting someone else. I had a friend who was already living there since our parents bought property together. She already had friends so I became a part of their group. I was determined to start fresh, but of course, a senior boy caught my attention and we started talking, a lot. I found myself sharing mostly about my old boyfriend and the breakup. He also shared about a girl he really liked but her parents wouldn't allow her to see him. We both were experiencing heartache.

It wasn't long before I gave myself away again. I was disappointed for letting it happen. Shortly after, I found out I was pregnant.

I was seventeen years old. He was eighteen. We were both afraid of what would happen, as we had no plans to marry. We barely knew each other. We began to argue about whether to have an abortion. I didn't want to, but I did consider it. He offered to make an appointment, but for once in my life, I felt like I had something to live for.

Although I was fearful of my parent's response and of what the future might hold for me, I wanted to carry this baby, my baby, and began to push the father away.

The thought of telling my parents was overwhelming. I knew they would be devastated. Our family was prominent in the church with my dad being a worship leader. I wanted to wait to tell them until I was further along. I needed more time to find a way. At the same time, my girlfriend was also expecting. She was further along and couldn't keep her secret any longer. Reluctantly, I agreed to tell our parents together. Our plan was to head to Seattle and stay with one of her friends while she left a note for her parents, which would naturally get to mine. Not exactly the plan I had in mind, but I went along with it. I did not leave a note and still to this day, I don't know what she wrote.

When we got to her friend's house, unannounced, my friend explained our situation. She let us in but only to call our parents, then said we should go back home. Her response was unexpected, but my friend called and spoke to her mom. As soon as she hung up, I drove us to my sister's apartment, not far from where we were. It was about ten o'clock at night. I told my sister of my pregnancy and she said we needed to call home. I didn't want to be the one to tell my parents so she did it for me. I'm pretty sure they already knew.

My parents were clearly disappointed at first. They had a vision for my future and news of my pregnancy made it seem as if all their hopes and dreams for me were suddenly *taken away*.

I spoke with my mom briefly. I don't remember exactly what she said, but I do remember she was more loving than I expected. I didn't speak with my dad, but I knew he was not happy. I had trouble falling asleep that night. Yet it was a huge relief knowing my secret was out.

When my friend and I finally arrived at my house, we were directed to sit at the family table. Our parents sat on each end. We both sat in the middle, heads hung in shame. There were words spoken, followed by an awkward silence. Our family dog broke the silence by lapping up water from her bowl. My friend and I could not hold back our nervous laughter. Our parents did not see the humor. In fact, it made them angry.

My friend went home with her parents and I ran to my room crying. My mom soon followed. I remember the sweater she was wearing that day. It had navy blue and green horizontal stripes, but it was my mother's soft voice telling me that everything was going to be okay that I remember the most. It wasn't long until my dad came around too.

At school, I soon went from the new girl to the pregnant girl. It was a small school and word got around quickly. There were only twenty-seven students in the entire junior class. I could feel the judgment from the other students and some of the school staff.

It didn't take long for morning sickness to kick in, which made it difficult to make it to my first class. I missed more than the maximum allowed days and did not receive credit. I could tell the teacher felt sorry for me and said he wished he could help, but he didn't make the rules.

I managed to pass my other classes, but there were times I had to leave in the middle of a lesson, run to the bathroom, and throw up.

Once I was reprimanded by a teacher for leaving without a hall pass. I felt like an outcast and couldn't wait to finish the school year. I could see the looks and hear the whispers as I walked the halls. Part of me didn't care because none of these people really knew me and I didn't care to know them, but it still wasn't a good feeling. Because the father and I were not on good speaking terms, it only added to the small-town drama.

At church, I felt like I made people uncomfortable, especially the youth pastor. Because of it, I quit going to youth service. Instead, I sat in church with my parents. For the most part, I felt supported by the leaders, but one thing has stuck with me all this time. Some of my mom's friends wanted to give me a baby shower, but the pastor wouldn't allow it to be at the church. He didn't want to give the impression they were condoning my behavior. I didn't hold it against him and asked him to baptize me a year later. It was hurtful, but at the time, I felt it was what I deserved.

As for my baby's father, I didn't feel he deserved to be involved because of his lack of support. It was clear in my mind that I would raise the baby while he could carry on with his life, but it was clouded thinking. His mom was brokenhearted and sent me flowers, cards, and letters. She wanted to be a part of the baby's life, but I just wanted to get through my first trimester.

After the father graduated high school, he ended up going into the military and was away for the birth. I felt relieved having distance between us, although I still felt overwhelmed by his mom wanting to be involved. At the time, I did everything in my power to avoid her.

I had so many emotions that took me different places on different days. It was daunting to say the least. I was dependent on my parents, and for the most part, I followed their lead, but they had a lot on their own plate. Dealing with the father and his family was too much for them to take on. I had five younger siblings and would soon find out my mom was expecting again. By the end of summer, we had moved again, but not very far away. I had plans to graduate high school and rather than sending me to public school, I was enrolled in an accredited program to complete my high school education. I finished a few weeks before my baby was born.

I didn't have an ultrasound prior to delivery because I used a midwife and planned a natural birth. Because of the lack of funds, it was my only option. I was anxious to know if I was having a boy or a girl. Once I got past the morning sickness, I loved being pregnant. Carrying a child for the first time was the most amazing experience—and then there was the birth. It was one of the hardest things I ever did. But I will never forget the moment my friend looked me in the face and said, "It's a *girl*."

I gave her a name which means *who is like our God*. She weighed a mere 5 pounds, 14 ounces. I will always remember the first time I held her in my arms and heard her cry. This was my baby girl and I was her mama. I would love her for all of my days.

The following months were difficult because nursing was painful and sleep was hard to come by. My mom was helpful, but she wasn't one to take over. She had her own flock to take care of. My recovery was prolonged because I became ill from mastitis. It took time to adjust to being a mom, especially since I was so weak. I needed help getting to and from the bathroom and blacked out more than a time or two. I was relieved when my parents agreed it was time to call it quits and let me put her on baby formula. Those first few months were much more challenging than I expected.

The father returned home before she was six months old and tensions rose again. This time it was about visitation. It was difficult for us to come up with a plan. I couldn't bear the thought of leaving my baby with his family. I was fearful of leaving her, but after a year or more of messy paperwork and attorney fees, things sort of died down. Over time, I began to see him and his mom in a different light. I grew more comfortable letting my daughter stay without me.

In the coming years, he would spend time with her when he was in town, mostly over the holidays. He lived in various places over the course of her life and throughout the years, he sent letters, books, and photographs.

It took a little convincing when I told my parents that I had decided to pursue my dream of going to college. Ultimately, they supported me, but were concerned about how much I could manage. My mom took care of my daughter while I attended classes and worked part time. Between cleaning homes and financial help from my grandmother, I didn't have to take out a school loan. I worked hard to complete my degree but still made time for a social life.

When I was twenty-one, I joined a singles group at another church and met some friends. As it turned out, they were more into partying than studying the Bible. On a Friday or Saturday night, I would put my daughter to bed and meet up with my new friends. We would drive up to Seattle and hit the clubs.

This led to a party phase that was short-lived, as were relationships, but it was hard for me to be alone. My daughter has always been a huge part of my life, which made it difficult to shield her from relationships. Sadly, I went from boyfriend, to boredom, to boyfriend, to heartache, to boredom, to boyfriend, to more heartache. I let life's distractions, such as social events, friends, and boyfriends, get in the way, but still managed to keep my grades up. It took two and a half years to complete my AA Degree in General Studies, but it was one of my greatest accomplishments.

After graduation, I had plans to move out. My sister and her husband bought a house and agreed to let me rent a room.

It was closer to where I grew up and it felt good being back in civilization. It was the right time to move since my mom and I were struggling to get along.

Our relationship improved when I took the leap. It was also the perfect time for my daughter, as she would begin kindergarten in the fall. I didn't want to raise her in a small town. It was also closer to the college I wanted to attend. I was accepted into the business program at the University of Washington, but it turned out I was short a class so I decided to work instead.

Rather than enrolling in school, I started my own business. I built up a clientele and continued to clean homes. I let my dream of finishing school rest and carried hopes of finishing someday in the future.

I also decided to get more involved with church—one that didn't have a singles group.

I first noticed my future husband at church while he was helping in my daughter's Sunday school classroom, but it wasn't until we were at a softball game that we were formally introduced. A couple months later, we started dating. We were inseparable and wanted nothing more than to get married—and less than a year later, we did. My daughter was six years old.

When my daughter was nine, we added to our family. I was twenty-seven and my husband was twenty-nine. We had a son. We found out we were expecting another child when he was about five months old. We didn't plan on having another baby so soon, but we were still happy. First, we were shocked. Then we were happy. One week before our son turned one, we had a daughter. We were razzed for having them so close together, and more than my husband, I was sensitive to the comments. It brought back feelings of not being accepted. I kept thinking, But I'm married this time.

About a year later, my daughter's biological father let my husband adopt her. The goal wasn't to push him away, but to release him from the child support and to let her officially change her last name. That piece of paper didn't change much else. My husband already thought of her as his daughter and her father wasn't discounted as her dad. Over time, her biological father and I have made amends. As our daughter grew older, he began to pursue a relationship with her, and their relationship continues to grow to this day.

As the years went by, as a wife and stay-at-home mom, I struggled with feelings of inadequacy, which eventually led to a struggle with perfectionism. I put too much importance on a clean and tidy home. I wanted to be seen as a good wife, and saw that as the way to prove myself. When my husband didn't notice, I would become defensive when his reaction didn't meet my expectation. I told myself, "I'm not a good enough wife. I need to be a better mom." Behind closed doors, I was an emotional mess.

I finally decided to start seeing a counselor. I learned a lot about myself in therapy, but it didn't take away my problems—much like marriage didn't take away loneliness or insecurity. It only made it more visible. I learned that my fear of rejection was heavy and that I carried a great deal of shame. In order to experience healing, I was told I needed to walk in my pain, but instead, I began to run…literally.

I'm not sure if I was running from my problems, but it sure felt good not having to deal with them. I ran my first mile in the dead of winter and was determined to keep on going. I started by signing up for my first 5K and a subscription to Runner's World magazine. I followed one of the training plans and worked my way to a 10K and eventually the half-marathon distance, but I knew I wanted to go further.

As I ran, I took the opportunity to grow personally while also growing closer to God. Between the songs on my iPod and my dependency on God, I faced my fears and pushed through when it felt too difficult. My daughters even joined me on my longest training run. My teenager got out her bike and pulled her sister along beside me.

Mentally, I knew that if I could run 26.2 miles, I could also handle going back to college. School remained a constant in my mind. Yet there were so many things that made pursuing a degree feel impossible: finances, time, being a mom, being a wife. When I finally crossed the finish line after a whole year of training, it was the most amazing feeling. I accomplished something I never thought I could. I ran a full marathon! I was proud of myself and so was my family. Ultimately, it was a jump-start to pursuing my dream of going back to school, a dream I thought had been *taken away*.

I will never forget the day I received my acceptance letter from the University of Washington. It was a beautiful summer day. My husband had just brought in the mail. I couldn't seem to open the letter, so I let him do it. I was glad to discover his tears were happy ones. As for myself, I was terrified. I wasn't sure what I was getting myself into.

I enrolled in school full time.

I continued to spread myself a little too thin. Between my family, church activities, school, and the gym, it felt like I was drowning. My husband alleviated responsibilities by filling in the gaps with household tasks and our family routine. I couldn't have done it without him.

Over winter break, I hit an all-time low and began to see my counselor again. Not long after, I started taking medication.

> I took the opportunity to grow personally while also growing closer to God.

It was a difficult choice, but it helped me out of the depression I was in. Music also helped me through, and many times my husband held me while I cried.

After a ton of work and a few emotional breakdowns, I graduated from the University of Washington with a Bachelor of Arts degree in Media and Communication Studies and Society, Ethics, and Human Behavior. My family should have earned a degree too for helping me make my dream a reality. I was elated when my diploma arrived in the mail and I officially became a Dawg! I completed my degree within a week of my daughter graduating high school.

It was an exciting time for both of us, but bittersweet as a mom.

Prior to my daughter's graduation, I felt like I was losing a part of myself. I was having a difficult time letting go, especially since she would be leaving in the fall. My daughter knew I was struggling and shared Scripture verses from Isaiah 43: *But now, this is what the Lord says - he who created you, O Jacob, he who formed you, O Israel; "Fear not, for I have redeemed you; I have summoned you by name; you are mine. When you pass through the waters, I will be with you and when you pass through the rivers, they will not sweep over you. When you walk through the fire, you will not be burned; the flames will not set you ablaze. For I am the Lord your God, the Holy One of Israel, your Savior."*

It was her way of saying that God would be with her wherever she goes.

The following weekend, I was scheduled to attend a women's retreat. I didn't want to go, as I was in a slump, but felt obligated since I was on the women's ministry team. The weekend was lined up with speakers sharing powerful stories, but it wasn't until the last day that God spoke to my heart, in more ways than one. It was through the speaker. She began by reading out of Isaiah 43, the same Scripture verses my daughter had given me for comfort, so it caught my attention. It was as though God was telling me the same thing. My daughter was in His hands.

The speaker also talked about her past and the freedom she experienced through letting go. When she finished speaking, I sat in my seat for a while just thinking, What do I need to let go of? I knew I needed to trust that God was in control, but I felt a burden deeper within. She said if anyone needed prayer, she would be available up front. I decided to get up and ask for prayer. Before she prayed, she asked, "So what is it you need to let go of?" My first thought was guilt and shame, but when I opened my mouth, out came, "I don't know." She then asked if it was guilt and shame and I said, "Yes." I couldn't help but cry. I felt so broken, and yet so loved by God. The speaker didn't know what I was holding onto, but God did. He knew what was tucked away in my heart and wanted me to let it go. When I finally did, my burden was *taken away.*

Although I knew God most of my life, it was in that moment, I realized just how much He knew me. He wasn't holding my past against me, like I had been. He was the only one who could *take away* all the hurt I was carrying.

Do I still experience pain? Yes. Do I still care a little too much about what others think of me? I wish I could say no. Do I still find myself trying to do things perfectly? At times I do, but God will continue to use my struggles and even my failures to bring me back to Him. I am learning to accept the grace He has for me and it is a beautiful thing.

God has a purpose for my life and for my daughter's life. Being a teen mom was hard. My daughter had to be part of much of my struggle as I went through my ups and downs. Yet, I am so very proud of the woman she has become. She recently married a great guy we all love.

My husband and I have been married for fifteen years now. It hasn't always been easy. We are both in need of God's grace. We still have some growing to do, and although we have faced many ups and downs, it has only made us stronger. Over the years, I have come to realize that my husband wasn't meant to complete me, but to be a companion.

Through my journey I have learned that following God isn't about wearing a mask or a "church smile" to make people believe everything is okay, it's about being honest with myself and trusting God to heal my broken places. No longer do I see what I've done, but what He has done.

I don't have everything together and it's doubtful I ever will, but I belong to God. He is with me too. He's always been with me, not just when I walked into the doors of a church, but when I walked out too. He was with me when I promised to follow Him wholeheartedly for the hundredth time and when I failed for the millionth. He is with you too. As a teen mom, you have enough to carry. If you are feeling the heavy

> God is waiting for you to turn to Him and let go of everything that is weighing you down or holding you back.

burden of guilt, shame, or even fear, as I was, my hope is that you will allow God to take it away. It took me a lot of years to realize it wasn't mine to carry. God is waiting for you to turn to Him and let go of everything that is weighing you down or holding you back. His grace is enough for you...

What is it that you need to let go of? What burden are you carrying that needs to be *taken away*?

...the one who trusts in Him will never be put to shame.
                                    —Romans 9:33 (NIV)

I WILL TAKE CARE OF YOU

ABUSE AND ALCOHOLISM were part of my everyday life as far back as I can remember.

My mom tried very hard to give us happy memories. But they were obliterated by the horrible memories etched in my mind. We were a typical family—on the outside. We went to church, had a beautiful house, a nice car, and appeared to be living a normal American dream lifestyle.

However, within the four walls of our home, we were living an absolute nightmare.

My mom was the victim of extreme domestic violence, the kind most people only see in movies or hear about on the news. As a little girl, I took on the responsibility of the "mother hen" over my two younger siblings. I was their protector! When fights between my parents erupted, I would rush them to a room or hide them behind me as I called 911, screaming and begging them to hurry! My mom finally worked up the courage to leave my dad, which started a different sort of difficult chapter in our lives.

That led us from being homeless, to living in our car, and finally to staying in battered women's shelters. I have even been a recipient of Christmas presents from angel ministries seen in department stores during the holidays.

While we were living through this hell on earth, my dad was in prison. We often had to depend on food shelters for hot meals. Many times, we ate lunch from a brown paper bag handed out at the community park. This is one reason I thank God for the people who feel called to reach out to those in need. Due to my upbringing in the church, I always knew God was watching over us and He would help us get through anything. My siblings always looked to me for comfort, so I made them a promise. I promised them, *"I will always take care of you."*

Eventually, my mom remarried. That's when the terrible times really started. My stepdad was evil! He was a very mean man and I knew not to cross him or there would be hell to pay. I had no freedom, and as a preteen, I wasn't allowed to have a boyfriend. There were boys I liked, and boys who liked me. I wasn't even allowed to talk to them on the phone. He would threaten their lives if they called. At thirteen years old, he would still make me hold his hand in public and would tell me that if he caught me looking at boys, or them looking at me, he would destroy my face.

In the fall of 1994, we finally ran away. My mom took her final beating and we left my stepdad. Our life was again turned upside down. We were freed from a lost, angry, and abusive man and the mess of a life he was creating for us. But we were left, one more time, to figure out the details of how to survive.

Because my mom had never been allowed to work, she had no idea how to earn an income. We had no idea where we would live. We ended up in Fresno, California, because my mom knew two people there. She got a job working part time at a Burger King. This job provided just enough income to get a small apartment in the ghetto.

I thank God for the people who feel called to reach out to those in need.

It wasn't much, but it was better than the previous alternatives. The one-dollar Whoppers from Burger King were a huge blessing and might as well have been a fine meal in an upscale restaurant.

Being free from my stepdad was an incredible blessing for all of us, too. Unfortunately, along with this newly-discovered freedom, my mom began to party. My responsibility became greater as I continued fulfilling the promise I had made to my brother and sister:

"I will take care of you."

Eventually, I met a group of kids who belonged to gang families. They were just as messed up as mine. They all smoked weed and drank alcohol on a regular basis. Before I met them, I was a thirteen-year-old, straight A student who'd never been to a party or tried drugs. Now I was trying it all and going along with whatever would help me fit in with my new friends.

I would get high in the morning, make sure my brother was ready for school, walk my little sister to kindergarten, then go to school myself. While my mom was out, I would drink forties of malt liquor with my friends and smoke pot.

This became my daily routine.

On weekends, when my mom was home, I would be out partying all hours. If she wasn't home, I often took my little sister with me. Life seemed to be going great! I could feel all my worries fade away with weed and alcohol. I was clever enough to stay out of trouble, and I was having the time of my life. I hung out with a few different boys, even kissed a couple of them. Kissing was a huge deal to me after the destructive bubble I lived in.

Deep down, I knew this way of life was not okay, but I desperately wanted some semblance of belonging. I felt this group of friends saying to me, *"We will take care of you."* They created an environment of comfort, family, and fun. It felt good.

My life was an ongoing spiral of drugs, alcohol, and partying. Miraculously, I still managed to get straight As in school, and still kept up with all the responsibilities at home. I just figured out a way to balance everything and keep up the appearance that I had it all together.

Without warning, during the summer of 1995, my mom and her new boyfriend announced we were all moving to Washington State. I was born in Washington, and we'd visited there almost every summer to see my grandpa. I had friends there too, so I was excited to move and get away from the constant struggle in which we seemed to be living. I was relieved to have a fresh start!

I stuck out like a sore thumb at my new school. I was used to wearing the typical gangster clothing of California. Khaki Dickies, airbrushed shirts, bellbottoms, or mini-skirts with platform shoes. Not exactly the commonly-worn attire in my new Washington school.

My very first day of school, while being given a tour, a boy came up to me and asked my name. I politely answered and felt my heart skip a beat at the same time. Then doubt and confusion quickly swept in as I thought, *He's too normal for me.* He seemed like a sweet boy with slicked-back hair and nice clothes. I was used to the bad boys of California. This boy was not the type that interested me. However, something drew us to each other and after a short while, I ended up giving him my phone number.

Something was definitely missing in my life. My mom continued her pattern of one abusive boyfriend after another. Her partying got further and further out of control. She didn't even seem to care what we were doing, so we did what we wanted. I partied more, but still kept my promise and watched over my brother, my sister, and now my grandpa as well.

The boy I met on my first day of school was not my boyfriend. He was my saving grace. He would come hang out with my brother and he had such a sweetness about him that he grew on me. He would tell me that drinking and getting high wasn't something he liked and I found myself caring more about what he thought than going out to party.

It wasn't long before I was spending all of my time with him. Our parents trusted us, so we were allowed to have sleepovers and hang out all the time. As I got to know him better, I learned that his dad was an alcoholic and that had a lot to do with why he felt the way he did about drinking.

I loved spending time with him. He was my breath of fresh air. We were best friends and completely head-over-heels in love with one another. Eventually, we decided to take our relationship to the next level. I loved him. He loved me. We knew we wanted to be together forever.

We never even considered pregnancy was a possibility. It didn't seem feasible that something like that could happen to us. I was fifteen years old, and only weighed eighty-seven pounds. I suddenly found myself sick with flu-like symptoms every morning and couldn't figure out why.

Finally, my older sister asked me if I could be pregnant. My response was a very matter-of-fact, "No." She told me I needed to go to the doctor. She always teased me about being the angel of the family, because even though I often did bad things, I never got in trouble. The next day I went to Family Planning. I remember being in denial, and thinking there was no way I could be pregnant.

> We created this baby—therefore, we were going to take full responsibility for it.

The nurse at the Family Planning office was stern and showed no emotions as she drew my blood and took my urine sample. Her demeanor remained the same when she returned with the results. Her words seemed harsh as she questioned me about why I wasn't aware I was pregnant, and informed me I was approximately three months along.

I was shocked by the news and didn't know how to respond. I went to pick up my boyfriend from school and tell him the news. He turned pale and I thought for sure he was going to pass out. I felt the same way.

I knew telling my mom would be extremely difficult, so I just handed her the paperwork from the doctor's office with the positive pregnancy test attached. At first glance, she thought it was from my older sister. As soon as she realized it was mine, she just put her head down and cried.

We waited a week to tell my boyfriend's parents. As we expected, it didn't go over very well at all. His mom told us how stupid we were and that our lives were over. She told us we needed to have an abortion or give the baby up for adoption. I was so mad because those things weren't even an option to me. We created this baby—therefore, we were going to take full responsibility for it.

Once the news was out to all of our family and friends, we heard it all. Everybody seemed to have an opinion and know what was best for us. We were told we wouldn't be able to finish school, we would never amount to anything, it's impossible to be good parents at sixteen years old, and we would not be able to support ourselves. It was negative comment after negative comment from every direction.

I lost friends because their parents acted as if I was contagious and they thought I was a bad influence. But I was determined to finish school no matter what adversity life threw my way.

As my belly grew larger, I continued to work hard in school. I received weird looks and could hear whispers of judgment as I walked through the halls of my high school.

Two months before the baby was due, my doctor ordered me to bed rest. I was small, and my body wanted this baby out!

On May 18, 1997, I gave birth to a beautiful 7 pound, 12 ounce baby boy. My boyfriend was there for the entire labor and delivery. Shortly after our baby was born, he left to go to school. He wanted to stay, but he had gotten a job and was still in school full time. He was doing what he needed to do for us. As I gazed into the eyes of my precious son, I told him I would be the best mommy I could be. I told him that no matter what our future had in store, or how bumpy the journey might be, I promised him *"I will always take care of you."*

We knew it was going to take work, but we were both willing to do whatever was necessary for our son. At this point, our parents were supportive of our decision and they loved our baby. We loved each other, but the love we had for our son was unexplainable. He was so precious and innocent. This new life gave me a new sense of hope for my future. We were able to spend all summer with him, but going back to school in the fall was the hardest thing I ever had to do. I was sixteen years old, nursing a baby, and starting my junior year of high school. I had to go. We had to go. We had to finish high school! We didn't give ourselves another option.

It wasn't easy. I remember how difficult it was as I struggled through my last period class, my breasts leaking milk through my shirt. I was so embarrassed. But this was my reality and I didn't have another choice.

My teenage body learned to function on very little sleep. I would wake up at five in the morning to get my baby and myself ready for the day. My boyfriend and I were both full-time students and as soon as school was over, we would head to work until eleven at night. We did what we had to do for our son, and to survive. This journey was extremely difficult, but it made both of us stronger.

The start of our senior year finally arrived! Our son was now almost two years old. We faced many obstacles as teen parents. At one point, our parents thought it would be best to keep us away from each other—that maybe it would prevent another pregnancy. Their attempts to keep us apart failed. We loved each other and we were not going to be kept away from each other. We learned our lesson and we

Parenting while still living with your own parents is extremely difficult!

didn't want another baby just yet. But it was hard work being a parent.

One day, out of the blue, my boyfriend's mom decided we should have a parenting plan in place. I was extremely upset! He could see our son as often as he wanted, and we had a great relationship. His mom wanted a plan established just in case anything went wrong in our relationship. I understood that we were young and she was trying to protect her son from heartache, yet it was still hurtful.

The night before Valentine's Day, my boyfriend called me and demanded that he get to keep our son overnight. I was confused. He had never taken him from me and suddenly he wanted him overnight? I was a wreck. To this day I have never forgotten the anger I felt. I had never felt hatred towards my boyfriend, but that night I did. We worked through it the next day and realized it was more of a power trip from his mom, and it was pointless. Parenting while still living with your own parents is extremely difficult!

We graduated high school in 1999. It was not an easy journey, but definitely worth it! It was a huge accomplishment for both of us. We bought our first house right out of high school and on our five-year dating anniversary, he proposed! He told me how he knew the moment we met in junior high, that I would be the one he would marry.

I felt something special that day too. I felt so blessed when my best friend asked me to marry him. It was not going to be an easy journey, but we knew we weren't walking alone. God had been there, walking alongside of us the entire time. God guided me and kept me safe through all of my childhood struggles. He placed an incredible boy in my path at just the right time to change the destructive course I was on of drugs and alcohol. God blessed us with our perfect son. God forgave us of our sins, strengthened us along the way, and taught us to love through every circumstance.

On our wedding day, I received another amazing gift from God. The day I became a wife was also the day a relationship with my dad began to be restored.

He was released from prison and made sure to be at my wedding, to walk me down the aisle. That was such a great blessing! My dad wasn't a bad person. He was a real person who made some bad choices and served his time for them. My dad believed in God, and because we are human, we sometimes stray from God's path.

From that day forward, my relationship with my dad grew. He became a grandpa to my kids, and the dad I always wanted. He is still an active part of our life and visits frequently.

After getting married, we became pregnant with our second son. I was excited, but I knew life would become harder. We were only nineteen and newly married. Our finances weren't the greatest, but they weren't terrible either. We had a mortgage, a car payment, and all of the other bills that come with having a family. I didn't worry because we never went without. I specifically remember writing checks to pay all of our bills after the birth of our second son and ending with a balance of $17. Praise God and my husband for always providing!

More important than having money, we were always happy, our boys were always happy!

During this time, my mom became engaged, and she was back to her original self. The mom I knew and prayed she could be, the best grandma ever. She helped take care of our babies and they loved her. She was the grandma who would bake for them, let them play in the dirt, and give them her undivided attention. She still struggled with alcohol a little, but you could see her light shining through.

We bought our second home a couple of years later and I started a home business I still do to this day. I'm a very lucky mom. I get to work and provide an income by staying home with my boys. Life is very good! I believe I have the life I do because of the adversity I went through when I was younger. I know I am a better person, and a stronger person, because of it. God had an amazing plan for my life. I believe He was watching over us during everything we went through. The good, the bad, and the ugly. The hardships we survived taught us so much and we plan to change lives for God's glory because of it.

Always know God has a plan for you. God can take any situation and work it for His glory. Through every struggle, my husband and I worked together, with God's help, to overcome it. We always leaned on our faith, and we built our foundation on God. We struggled, but never stopped loving each other. We've never broken up, or even discussed separation or divorce. We both firmly believe we are in this 'till death do us part.

> the storm God brought us through was preparing us for all the beautiful things that were yet to come.

I believe, without any doubt, that the storm God brought us through was preparing us for all the beautiful things that were yet to come. I am a very blessed mama, now raising four sons. I have an incredible man by my side with whom I get to celebrate twenty years of being together, fifteen of that in marriage.

God is so faithful to His Word. He fills every void. He reminds me in every situation I face..."*I will take care of you!*"

God is our refuge and strength, an ever-present help in trouble.
—Psalm 46:1 (NIV)

YOU ARE NOT ALONE

MY MOTHER WAS young—only seventeen years old when she first held me in her arms. Even though I'm sure she loved me, she wasn't ready to grow up, or to be a mother. She was still trying to find herself, who she was, and learn how to be an adult.

I didn't meet my father until later in life. He left before I was a year old, to join the military.

When I was three, my mother moved us to Albuquerque, New Mexico. She loved the party life and quickly became addicted to drugs and alcohol. She also loved being the center of attention. Shortly after our move she met a man who enjoyed a similar lifestyle, and they married. By the age of four, I had seen way more than any child should ever see. I learned to call the police after several episodes of both parents being drunk and starting to fight.

I lived in constant fear. I felt *alone.*

My mother's drinking and drug use progressed. She became addicted to heroin and left my stepfather for her addictions. She began working as a prostitute to earn drug money and money to support us. I would often sit in the car, alone, for hours, and watch her go into room after room with her "dates."

Eventually she started developing mental issues and heard voices. She would carry on full conversations with the walls and a blank TV. I was so scared. My mother, who once played Barbie with me and tucked me in at night, was no longer the same person. I felt as though I were living with a complete stranger.

As my mother's addiction progressed, she started "slamming her dope." She began hanging out with a very scary group of people from the Hell's Angels motorcycle gang. Her new boyfriend would make me sit in a room by myself and throw lunchmeat on the floor for me to eat.

There were times I would go days without eating, or even seeing sunlight.

One day, he held me by my neck and made me watch my mother stick a needle in her arm to get high. I hated him. I hated him even more when he would have his way with me when my mother was passed out.

I lost so much of my childhood because of the choices my mom made, and the things I was forced to experience.

No child should ever experience those things. No child should ever feel *alone*.

By the grace of God, Child Protective Services (CPS) came by my school to pick me up. I was finally removed from my mother's care. I was now safe...supposedly. This began my journey through the foster care system.

The first home I was placed in was with a lady who was very nice, but all I wanted was my mother. So at eight years old, I ran away to find her. I was picked up by the police and placed in a different home. After being bounced around to four other foster homes, I was taken in by a family who sexually abused me.

I ran away again.

> I lost so much of my childhood because of the choices my mom made, and the things I was forced to experience.

The foster care system finally realized I would continue to run away, so at the age of nine, I was placed in my first lockdown children's institution. I responded surprisingly well to the discipline and structure I was given there. It was the first time I felt the warmth of security and boundaries that every child needs.

My short stay at the institution ended when my aunt and uncle fought for and got custody of me. They became my heroes—but they had no idea what they would be dealing with. They probably thought they were getting a sweet, ten-year-old girl, who loved princesses and played with toys. Sadly, at ten years old I had already learned how to lie, steal for survival, manipulate people to get what I wanted, and rebel against help from others because I had been taking care of myself and my mother for so long.

I desperately wanted to love and be loved. I just didn't know how. I was rebellious, angry, resentful, sad, hurt, and filled with pain. I was constantly getting kicked out of school for fighting, so my uncle would send me away to my grandma's.

My grandmother was also my hero, but I had no idea how to respond to her love and continued to rebel. When she couldn't handle me, I would be sent back to my aunt and uncle. This caused a cycle of rejection. I blamed everyone else for how I behaved and took no responsibility for my actions.

I wish now I could just go back and listen to what they tried to teach me. That's why I'm sharing my story. Maybe, just maybe, I can reach a young girl who has suffered so much, and needs to know this one thing: *You are not alone.*

Eventually, my need for love and attention led me to get it from boys.

I started having sex when I was thirteen years old. I enjoyed it. I liked being touched. In a sick way, it was familiar, and I felt important. My aunt and uncle tried so hard to keep me in positive things like sports and church, but I just wanted to do my own thing, and they struggled to stop me.

I was fifteen years old and living with my boyfriend, when I found out that I was pregnant—and honestly, I was so happy! I can remember thinking: *Finally, I will know what it's like to have that mother-child bond back! A baby will love me, and I will love my baby.*

My family was not okay with my decision and offered abortion or adoption as my options.

I just couldn't imagine giving my baby away, and I wasn't going to kill it. My unborn child's father was an irresponsible, "wannabe gangsta" who cared more about smoking pot, and getting into trouble, than he did about being a father. I was determined not to be the kind of mother my mom was to me. So I left him.

I soon found a home for at-risk teen moms, where I would be living with other moms. I was so thankful for this place. The couple that ran it had a very strong faith in God. They were always telling us how we could find refuge in God, that He could make us new, and that He loved me and would forgive me if I asked Him to. I remember the woman once telling us that we were held accountable for our actions by God from as early as when we knew how to lie. All I could think of was all the bad things I had done. I wondered how God could love or forgive me, after all of that.

One evening, I accepted Jesus into my life in a way that was real to me. I remember one night, after getting into a huge argument with my baby's father, and knowing that he was not going to be the man or father I wanted him to be, I cried out to God. Honestly, it was more out of anger then it was for help. "Why God, why *me?* Why am I *alone* again?"

I will never forget the love I felt that day. It was like a blanket of peace and joy. And for the first time, I had an encounter with Jesus. A vision. It was I, a little girl, wearing a white dress, swinging on a tree swing. In my vision, I remember Jesus telling me to just play and rest because my Father was there. I cried and cried and asked Jesus to live in me, and forgive me of all my wrong doings, and help me to live better. I was talking to Him as if He was my friend and was right next to me… and He was.

It was then that I heard the words, *"You are not alone."*

When it was time to give birth to my son, I was in labor for three days! I pushed for five hours, and was in serious pain. He was 8 pounds, 11 ounces, and 21 inches long. He was so handsome, and perfect…except they discovered he had an irregular heartbeat. Three hours later, they wanted to separate me from my baby and take him to another hospital.

They sent in social workers, and were concerned with my abilities to care for my baby being a teen mother. They started to talk to me about adoption. I was so angry. No way! This was *my* baby! God gave him to me! So I went to the hospital where he was, against my doctor's orders. I had lost a lot of blood, and they wanted to keep me there.

However, there was no way I could be away from my son and leave him *alone;* after all, I knew exactly what that felt like.

Finally, after two weeks of being in the hospital we were able to go home.

I went to live with my aunt and uncle. My family began to see I was determined to be a good mother and take care of my baby. My grandma came and stayed with me for a couple of weeks to help me out. She was such a treasure in my life!

At sixteen, I moved out and got my own place. I also got into another relationship. I wanted desperately to have my own family, but I was still just a child myself. I saw all my friends going to school, playing sports, going to parties, and hanging out. Very quickly I was "that girl" who was called a "whore" and a "slut" and talked about because I had a baby.

Sadly, some of those same girls who judged me were girls whose hands I'd held through their abortions. This hurt badly, and made me angry. Eventually, I isolated myself. I dropped out of school and got my GED. I was working two to three jobs to pay my bills.

Since I couldn't go out to parties, my house became the party house. I started drinking at night after I would put my son to bed. My boyfriend at the time was only seventeen. He wanted us to be a family, and worked a part-time job. However, he also liked smoking weed. He would sell it on the side to support our habit and make a little extra money.

Then, like most bad decisions, it eventually got worse. Our seemingly innocent weed addiction turned into 'shrooms, then 'shrooms turned into ecstasy, and things continued spiraling downward.

At eighteen, I was pregnant again—this time with a baby girl.

My boyfriend and I both tried to clean up our act. We stopped using drugs and moved to a different town to start over. My boyfriend got a better job and so did I. We tried to make things work, but we fought all the time.

I soon found out he was being unfaithful to me and also using drugs again. This time, he was using meth. I left him.

At nineteen, I found myself on my own with two kids. I worked two jobs to make ends meet, and had daycare raising my kids. It was hard and stressful. Even though I loved my kids, I once again found myself feeling very *alone.* It was a reoccurring theme in my life.

> I knew God was trying to get my attention, and behind bars was the only place the drugs couldn't find me.

Around this time I had an older friend, who looked a lot like me. When I found out that I could pass as her, we started going out to the bar together on the weekends. I'd work all week away from my kids, then felt like I deserved to go out.

In no time at all I was drinking almost every night. I began sleeping around, seeking love, and searching for anything to fill my emptiness.

This went on for a couple years.

Finally, I ran into my daughter's father. He told me that he'd changed and was clean. We decided to get back together and try to make our relationship work.

Two months later I once again discovered he was lying. He was not only using drugs, but selling too. I also found his stash of cocaine. I was filled with emotions: anger, confusion, and fear, but curiosity got the best of me. So all by myself, I tried cocaine for the first time, and I liked it. I hated myself for liking it. I felt like I had just lost the battle of life, becoming everything I said I would never be.

I was becoming my mother. I hated her, and now I hated myself.

I continued to use cocaine daily. I completely lost myself in my drug addiction. I felt empty and *alone*. I started hanging out with the wrong people. Scary biker people, just like my mother did. I would drop my kids off with family for days, sometimes weeks at a time, or drag them with me from place to place.

My grandmother spent many days and many nights on her knees praying for me. She loved my children and me, and always understood the power of prayer.

I spent the years of 2002 and 2003 in and out of jail with many different convictions. Every time I was behind bars, I would sober up enough to feel a tug on my heart. I knew God was trying to get my attention, and behind bars was the only place the drugs couldn't find me.

Every time I would pray and promise that it was going to be different, that I was going to be a better mom, and I was going to get my life together. I wanted to be who I once was—a responsible, loving mother to my children. However, I didn't understand addiction. I did nothing to seek help or learn how to stay sober. I wanted things to change, but didn't take the steps necessary for change to happen. I would get out and continue to hang out at the same places, with the same people, and it wouldn't be long until I would start using drugs again.

I let meth control my life, and I wasn't strong enough to stop it. I liked the way it made me feel and would do anything to get it.

At age twenty-three, the justice system finally got tired of seeing me. They wanted me to turn in the people I was associated with. In the world I was living in, that was a very dangerous thing to do, so I refused. I kept silent. Because of that, I was sentenced to thirty-three months in state prison.

Although I was devastated, this really was an answer to many prayers. My kids were separated and placed into each of their fathers' families, while I sat behind bars, detoxing. I was scared, embarrassed, humiliated, and hopeless. However, prison was the very thing that would save my life.

Prison was degrading at first. People were in my face all the time, telling me I was worthless, that my life didn't matter, and that once I went to prison I would keep going back. I felt trapped once again.

The first forty-five days I spent in a holding cell with another woman for twenty-three hours a day. I got one hour out to shower or make a call. The only thing in the room was a Bible and a deck of cards. Days went by that all I could do was stare at that dusty book. I was actually angry towards God. I felt like He had left me. How could He allow me to have made the choices I had made?

Finally, out of boredom, I picked up the Bible and began to read the New Testament. I would pray, "God if You are real, then prove it."

Slowly, I started to feel the tug on my heart again. I started remembering songs I learned in church and would sing. I was worshiping Him through my singing and didn't even realize it. My heart began to soften and God began to work on me.

After forty-five days, I was shipped to a maximum-security prison to be evaluated as a violent offender. Since they could see the change in me, I was sent to a minimum-security facility. I couldn't believe my eyes when we pulled up. It was beautiful! I was in awe of the majestic-looking

> I was no longer just desiring change to happen, but I was walking out the steps to make it happen.

trees. My heart fluttered at the sight of deer across the street and a family of raccoons climbing in a tree.

Women in the facility were wearing their own clothes instead of state-issued uniforms. I was assigned a dorm and given a schedule. There were plenty of things to do there, but one of the first things I did was check out a church service. At the first service I attended, I listened to the pastor preach about spiritual gifts.

Halfway through the service he called me up to the front of the church. I was nervous, especially being the brand new girl. What he said to me that day blew me away.

He said, "Young lady, I have a message for you from your God." Tears began streaming down my face as the pastor spoke what he heard. "Your Father God says, *I have placed you here for a reason. I know the plans I have for you. You have been set apart to do My Kingdom's work. I love you daughter, and you are not alone.*" All I could do was lift my hands to heaven and surrender to Him. I was ready for change, and knew I was no longer going to be doing it on my own. I was given a new strength and new hope.

For twenty-seven months I worked on me. I began to understand that even though God loves me and has a plan for me, He also gives us free will. It was my decisions that had gotten me into this mess, not God.

I checked myself into a voluntary behavior modification treatment program. I learned all about trauma, co-dependence, chemical dependency, addiction, and abandonment. I learned how drugs and alcohol were not my problem, but that my thoughts, actions, and behaviors were the problem. I learned about Alcoholics Anonymous and Narcotics Anonymous. I learned how there were people on the outside where I could find fellowship, and find support amongst other addicts who were on a similar road to recovery.

I worked hard on myself, and slowly watched as my life began to transform. I was no longer just desiring change to happen, but I was walking out the steps to make it happen.

During my time in prison, I had no contact with my children. I prayed every day that God would protect them and soften their hearts to forgive me. So many times I cried because I missed them, and I worried they would have bitterness in their hearts, like I had for my mother.

My relationship with God continued growing stronger. I wrote in a journal and read my Bible every day. I felt happiness flooding my heart, and didn't feel *alone* anymore.

God did for me what no person and no drug could do. He restored me and shed His grace on me. He filled that empty spot in my heart that I had tried, without success, for years to fill on my own with sex and drugs. He forgave me, and I was able to forgive me too. I was even able to forgive my mother, which was something I never thought would be possible.

After being in prison for twenty-eight months, I finally received word that I was going to be transferred to a work release program. It was like Christmas! I was finally going to be in a place that would begin allowing me to re-enter the community. I would be able to see my family, and begin looking for work and housing. I couldn't wait to see my children!

I entered the work release program with a plan to create a much different life. I attended meetings, stayed sober, and plugged into church. I stayed away from the people I used to hang out with and didn't go to all the places that I used to. I chose to make changes that wouldn't take me back to that place of darkness and loneliness I had seen too many times.

I wanted so badly to become a new person and desired helping others do the same. What if, because of what I had walked through, I could help other women be the best moms they could be—live a life of freedom, and not have to go through all the things I went through?

This revelation quickly became my new life's mission. I got a job and found housing in the second-step housing program for women and children. Two months after moving in, my son came to live with me. What a miracle! He had so much love for me, and was so excited to be with me again. I continued looking for my daughter, but her father moved out of state with her. It took me several months and a lot of prayer to get her back.

> God truly has a plan for you and your baby's life.

Finally, we were reunited. Thank You, Jesus! I couldn't imagine living my life without her.

Along this journey I met many beautiful, strong, and courageous women who helped me, mentored me, prayed with me, and taught me how to become a better mother.

I am still learning and continuing to grow. I surrounded myself with people who modeled the lifestyle I wanted to live. My decisions to change my environment and seek God are ultimately the reasons I have not returned to prison, have my family back, and have stayed drug free.

I never gave up, and today I am able to live that changed life that I desired so deeply. I recently married a wonderful man, and together we have a son, and another son on the way. I also gained a stepdaughter who is eighteen. My son is now eighteen, and my daughter is fifteen. My children trust me, respect me, and they love me. They are my purpose and why I continue my fight to be better! They are the reason I get up every day and fight for my life, and why I have a burning desire to help other moms.

My kids are world changers and so am I! What if I would have listened to those people who told me to look at other options? What if I would have listened to those people who spoke all those negative things over me, and made me believe I was worthless? What if I wouldn't have picked up that Bible or given into that tug I had on my heart?

As I look back now, I can see all the ways God was always right there. He never left me *alone*.

You are reading my story for a reason! If there is anything I could say to you, it would be this: God truly has a plan for you and your baby's life. You are worth living a life of freedom, and I pray that you will experience real love and real joy. Never let people tell you that you can't, because you can! You are victorious! You are more than a conqueror. You have been redeemed! You are a Champion.

Most of all, *you are not alone.*

So do not fear, for I am with you;
do not be dismayed, for I am your God.
I will strengthen you and help you;
I will uphold you with my righteous right hand.

—Isaiah 41:10 (NIV)

A BETTER LIFE

MY BIRTH MOTHER was twenty-two years old when I was born. She didn't feel she was able to provide for me very well and she wanted more for me. She wanted me to have *a better life.*

God placed me with a loving Christian family when I was only two weeks old. I instantly had a mother, father, and six-year-old brother who loved me immediately and unconditionally. My mother was a stay-at-home mom while my dad worked nights. As I got older, I often accompanied her while she volunteered at my brother's school. He attended a Christian school at our church where we attended every Sunday. When I reached school age, I too, attended this school. We had a large yard where I would ride the tractor with my dad on the weekends. I had nothing less than a typical, functioning, happy family.

When I was five, my world was turned upside down. My parents divorced and everything changed. My mom, brother, and I moved out of the only house I had ever known, and in with my grandparents. I remember a lot of fighting and a lot of hurt. So much hurt that my brother made the decision not to see my dad anymore. I, however, continued visitations with my dad and the hurt and confusion lessened more and more as each year passed.

My parents continued to argue throughout the years about child support and custody, which landed them back in court several times. As

I grew older I started figuring out what I could and couldn't get away with at each household. My mom ran a much stricter household, whereas my dad was more lenient. I began playing my parents against each other to try and get what I wanted. If there was something my mom wouldn't get me, I would just go ask my dad and the answer was usually, "Yes."

I was still attending Christian school and desperately wanted to try public school. My cousin, who attended public school, was a huge influence on my desire to switch schools. I would see all of the friends she had, and all of the games and activities she was able to attend. The battle to attend public school began. My mom, of course, did not want me to change schools. She felt very strongly that the Christian school was the place I needed to be, and looking back, I understand why she wanted me there. She did everything she could to give me *a better life*.

I fought for what I wanted, which included getting my dad involved. After a lot of fighting and tears I finally got my way—I was going to public school.

I began seventh grade in public school. I excelled very quickly academically based on the fact I was so far ahead due to private school curriculum. It didn't take me long to make friends. I gravitated toward people who were a lot like me—clean-cut, good students. Everything was great and I was happy. My cousin, who was a year ahead of me in school, also went to this public school. It didn't take long for my circle of friends to start to change. I started meeting more people—a lot of them were a year older than me and many of them were boys. I enjoyed hanging out with the "older crowd" and I liked all of the attention I began getting from boys. My new circle of friends thought that smoking cigarettes and marijuana was the cool thing to do, so I began to do these things occasionally as well. I remained acquaintances with my old friends, but my new group began to take precedence. Despite my change in atmosphere at school, I remained a good student, never letting my grades fall.

I was fifteen as I began my freshman year of high school. I was introduced to new people through my crowd of friends. Some didn't go to my school. Some of them didn't go to school at all. During this time, my mother also remarried. I was not an advocate of her decision and my defiance only grew stronger. As ninth grade was wrapping up and summer began, I started spending a lot of time with these friends of friends. I was introduced to a boy, who used to date my cousin, so I already knew a little about him. He was attractive, nice, and knew how to say all of the right things. He hung around a rough crowd, but that didn't bother me. It didn't take long for phone numbers to be exchanged and we started talking every day. By the end of summer we were a couple.

My mom was not impressed. He was seventeen, had not completed ninth grade, was going to an alternative school, and didn't have a job. My mother did not want her daughter dating someone like this. I came up with every excuse I could think of to try and convince her that he was a nice boy and that he was the one for me. My dad was more receptive to the relationship. He decided to give my boyfriend the benefit of the doubt and accept him, at least until he proved him otherwise. My boyfriend's parents, however, accepted me with open arms. His father often reminded me how good for his son I was. My mother continued to try and convince me that my boyfriend wasn't good for me and made every effort to keep us apart. Despite her efforts, I was determined to keep dating him and would do whatever it took to see him.

Occasionally I told the truth and my mom knew I was going to see my boyfriend, but more often than not, I lied about where I was going and where I had been. My two best friends at the time were often my excuse for leaving the house. I led my mom to believe that I was with them.

One of these lies ended up backfiring on me.

I told my mom that I was staying the night at my friend's house and she told her mom she was staying at mine. We met up with our other friends—my boyfriend included—and went for a drive and smoked marijuana. We had no idea there was a gun in the car. We found this out when the police pulled us over. We all had to get out of the car with our hands up. The police promptly took my friend and me home. When the policeman rang the doorbell and my mom opened the door, I could see the worry and disappointment in her face. Before he left he told my parents and me that I was a good kid involved with the wrong crowd and reminded me that I was better than this. I continued to believe that my boyfriend was a good person and I wanted to be with

> I knew what the possible consequences were, but I didn't believe it could happen to me.

him. This incident, of course, caused my mom to be even stricter. She desired *a better life* for me.

My relationship with my boyfriend continued. We went to my tenth grade homecoming dance together and the longer we dated the more I wanted to be with him. We were in love. He would come meet me after school and we would talk for hours every night. This continued my entire sophomore year. Also, during my sophomore year I met my best friend. She was not completely impressed with my boyfriend, but accepted him for me. My boyfriend and I decided to take our relationship to the next level and started having sex. Sometimes we practiced safe sex and sometimes we didn't. I couldn't talk with my mom about this. She didn't even know I was seeing him most of the time and she had always told me: "You should never have sex before you are married." I knew what the possible consequences were, but I didn't believe it could happen to me.

I was wrong.

Summer was coming to an end when I started not feeling well. At this point, my cycle was pretty regular and I realized that I was a week late. I told my friend and she offered to go with me to buy a pregnancy test. We got to the store and I couldn't do it. She had to go in and buy it for me. My parents were at work so we went back to my house so I could take the test. I was nervous as I read the directions on the package. I took the test and it immediately read positive. I didn't know what to say, what to think, or what to do. I was scared. I was sixteen…and pregnant. My friend stayed there with me. At this point she was my rock and reminded me that everything would work out. I knew I needed to call my boyfriend and tell him the news. To my relief, he wasn't upset. He showed up at my house with a smile on his face, put his arms around my belly, and told me: "I'm glad you're pregnant, now I can keep you forever." I embraced this statement and accepted it as a reassurance that he loved me and that everything was going to be okay.

I decided to keep this news from my family for the time being. The next couple of weeks were brutal. I could not get the sinking feeling out of my stomach. I could not stop thinking about how my family would take the news and how others would judge me. I decided to confirm my pregnancy at Planned Parenthood and made a doctor's appointment for myself at another office. Planned Parenthood sent me home with many papers, some on pregnancy and others on abortion. I had already decided that neither abortion nor adoption were options for me.

I was now sixteen and driving. I was out and about with my boyfriend when my pager went off displaying my home phone number. I was close enough that I just drove home to see what my mother wanted. As I walked in the house she was sitting at the table with a strange look on her face, and I knew something was wrong. She looked at me straight in the eyes and asked "Are you pregnant?" I answered, "Yes." The doctor's office where I made my appointment had called to confirm my appointment. I was not there to answer the phone, but my mother had been. We did not exchange many more words and I immediately took my boyfriend home so I could come home and face my mother. I can't remember all of the words that were exchanged, but I do remember the look of hurt and disappointment in her face. I felt ashamed, very ashamed. My mom had called my grandmother in the meantime who arrived shortly after I got home. My grandmother immediately wrapped her arms around me and with tears in her eyes, told me everything was going to be okay and that she loved me very much. There was a lot of talking and a lot of tears that day.

My mom called my dad and told him the news as well. He did not take this news lightly. He was immediately angry. He urged me to get an abortion and said he would pay for it no matter what the cost. He advised me that I would not want a person like my boyfriend in my life for the next eighteen years. I told him that this option had already been presented to me and that it was not the right decision for my baby and me. I do not know my brother's initial thoughts about my situation. He was off at college when he found out, but he remained remarkably calm when I talked to him. He took a different approach than my father and urged me not to take adoption off the table yet. He reminded me how young I was, how hard it might be, and how a family who can't have children may be able to give my baby *a better life*.

My brother and I, both being adopted, know firsthand what a blessing an adopted child can be. I remember telling him I would not forget adoption as an option, but deep down I knew that I wanted to keep my baby. I told my mom, dad, and grandma that this is what I wanted. My father and I stopped talking for a long time after this—the fact that he wouldn't speak to me made me feel even more ashamed. Although my family was embarrassed, disappointed, and saddened by the situation, I knew that they, other than my father, would be there for me through this pregnancy and would support whatever decision I made in the coming months.

It was my junior year...and I was pregnant. Not many people knew and I feared that the day I started showing, everyone would know. What would they think? How would they react? My teachers would be so disappointed. How was I going to make it through this year? There were so many thoughts circulating rapidly through my mind. I was not well for the first few months of my pregnancy. I was sick every morning and randomly throughout the day. Often, I would have to step out of class because I was sick and eventually had to tell my teachers that I was pregnant. So of course classmates started asking questions and people knew long before I wanted anyone to.

I did not receive as negative of a reaction as I had anticipated, especially from classmates. People were supportive and didn't seem to look down on me. My teachers made efforts to work with me and I no longer had to make excuses about why I was leaving class. This, however, did not lessen any embarrassment I held inside. I was back in school, getting up every morning and doing homework every night. I began to feel a lot of resentment toward my boyfriend. He did not attend school, and therefore, would go out with his friends every night. I would talk to him every day and see him after school and on the weekends, but I knew, every night after we ended our conversation he would be out again, doing whatever he wanted to do. How was this fair? I was the one who was sick every day and had to get up and go to school. My mom came to all of my doctor appointments with my boyfriend attending only a few.

I remember the day I found out I was having a girl—one of the few times I was actually excited about having a baby. My mom and family seemed excited too. There was no hiding it anymore. It was becoming very apparent that I was pregnant. The looks that I received from random kids at school didn't bother me, but the looks I received from adults killed me. I could see them judging me, and I remember thinking, If they only knew how they

> I was determined to graduate and not become a statistic just because I was having a baby.

were making me feel right now. Do they not realize how awful I feel already? I'm a pregnant teenager for goodness sakes! I dreaded going to my job at Shopko because every shift I would have to deal with many adults looking down on me. My boyfriend eventually got a job there too. I was able to see him more and it felt like he was taking a step in the right direction preparing for us to be a family. My boyfriend's father had talked a lot about marriage. My boyfriend had reassured me that this is what he wanted too. To my surprise, as my boyfriend and I were spending some time together at the park, he got down on one knee and asked me to marry him. I didn't say yes right away; I didn't know what to say. What would my mother say if I came home with a ring on my finger? I was only seventeen. I couldn't get married yet. After much thought, I decided that maybe that is what God wanted, maybe that was the right thing to do and I said yes. My mother did eventually see the ring, but I had not mentioned that it was an engagement ring; I let her believe it was a promise ring.

I continued going to school. This was something that was very important to me. I was determined to graduate and not become a statistic just because I was having a baby. I was about to become a mom so graduation was pertinent. I needed my high school diploma in order to go to college so I could get a good job and support this baby I had decided to bring into the world. It was the only way I knew how to create *a better life* for us.

I met with the school counselor who suggested I look into an alternative school because it had a daycare. Reluctantly, I followed

I was a seventeen year old little girl, holding a beautiful baby in my arms who was dependent on me.

his advice. I made an appointment and checked out the alternative school. When I arrived they had me take a test to see where I was academically. It was evaluated while I was there and I only missed two on the entire test. The counselor there informed me that I didn't need to be a student there and there were other options. I was put in touch with a program through my high school. After my baby was born I would be able to do contract classes. I would be able to take all of my normal classes, but would be able to do my work at home, and still receive my diploma from my current high school.

Things were looking up.

My due date came and passed. I went into labor three days after she was due. I called my boyfriend to come and get me. I was still living with my mom and stepdad, and he with his parents. He took me to the hospital and they sent me home. My boyfriend stayed with me until I had contractions so bad that he took me back in. This time they kept me. I had so many thoughts running through my head; pretty soon I was going to be a mother.

Labor was long, twenty-two hours with two hours of pushing. Unfortunately, my labor was not progressing, and I had to have an emergency C-section. I was exhausted and I decided to be sedated during the delivery. When I woke up, I was a mother. I was a seventeen year old little girl, holding a beautiful baby in my arms who was dependent on me. I was in awe of how tiny and perfect she was. My age didn't matter anymore. I was her mommy. I was now in charge of another human life. I could see the happiness in my boyfriend's face. We were going to do this; we were going to be a family. For a moment, it seemed as if everything was going to work out.

After spending three days in the hospital it came time to take this tiny baby home. One matter that had not been discussed was with whom I was going to go home after the baby was born. My boyfriend and his parents wanted me to go home with them. My mother wanted me to come home with her and my stepdad. Nobody seemed concerned about asking me what I wanted. The fight escalated and security was called to the maternity floor and eventually the police. It was decided that I go home with my mother. I felt a sense of relief.

The first couple of weeks were hard, but my mother was there to help me. I was sore from the C-section and I was exhausted. My mother let my boyfriend visit frequently. My boyfriend told me how much he missed me and how much he wanted to be there for our daughter and me. He wanted us to come live with him at his parents' house. I was quickly convinced that this is what I wanted as well. The three of us needed to be together. It only took a couple of weeks and against my mother's wishes, I moved in with my boyfriend and his family. It was a very awkward time and I wasn't comfortable there. I spent a lot of time in the bedroom with the baby and doing my schoolwork. My boyfriend's mother was very kind. She cooked all of my meals. They tried to make me feel comfortable, but I never really was. The possibility of getting married still weighed on my mind and truly, this is what I thought was the right thing to do.

We were married two months after our daughter was born. The ceremony took place at the courthouse where my mother had to sign because I was still a minor. It had taken a lot of convincing to get her to sign the papers. There were a lot of tears that day. I cried through the entire ceremony. At that moment I had doubts, but I still thought it was the right thing to do.

For a little while things were good. We moved into our own apartment. We qualified for low-income housing at the time. We both continued to work at Shopko and I continued my studies. I made it through my senior year, married with a child. I was very proud as I walked with my class at graduation, with my best friend as my partner. I always had planned to go away to a four-year college. However, this wasn't an option anymore. It was time to make a decision about what I was going to do with the rest of my life. During the year following graduation, there were many arguments. He still wanted to go out with his friends and he did. I would occasionally go out as well. We would argue about where each other had been or whom we were with; it was a very juvenile marriage. I knew I wanted more. I knew I needed more in order to raise my daughter. I was beginning to mature and stay true to myself. The person, deep down, I had always been.

I began looking into what our local community college had to offer. I knew if I stayed local, I would have the help I needed from my family to balance school and motherhood. I applied for and received student loans and grants. Nine months after high school graduation I began taking classes at the local community college. I looked into the programs the college had to offer. I did some job shadowing and chose a program to work towards. While in college I began to see and talk to friends I hadn't communicated with in a long time, most of them knowing my history. I also began to make many new friends with similar goals and ambitions. My father and I also recovered our relationship. This felt amazing. I no longer felt embarrassed; I felt strong and accomplished. This determination shed a new light on my future.

My daughter's father and I grew apart. We both loved our daughter very much, but our interests and goals were no longer a commonality. I filed for divorce a few months after starting college when our daughter was just a little over one year old. This brought forth a feeling of sadness for me, but also a sense of relief. It was a new beginning.

My family was there for me every step of the way. There were arguing and disagreements during the divorce, making me thankful our daughter was too young to realize what was going on. During the separation my daughter and I moved back in with my parents. She continued to see her father every other weekend. I still felt resentment toward him. The fact that he was able to do whatever he wanted except for every other weekend angered me. I was the one working, taking our daughter to and from daycare, and going to school. I felt like I was the only one trying to make a life for myself so I wouldn't have to struggle to care for my child. I didn't understand why he didn't want the same for himself. I knew what I needed to do and hoped he would find his own way to succeed.

One of the people I reconnected with at the community college was one of my best friends from middle school. We had remained acquaintances in high school, but had very different friends. He was taking classes at the community college with plans to transfer to a university. He knew my story, and we began talking every day. We quickly became good friends again and not long after we became a couple. God brought him into my life at the perfect time. He was very encouraging, supportive, and wonderful with my daughter. He accepted her, along with my past, and so did his family. I learned what true love really was and what a healthy relationship was truly about. I was accepted into the radiology program and he was accepted to a university three hours away. He moved away while I stayed local and we continued our relationship long distance with frequent trips to visit each other. My daughter and I eventually moved out into our own apartment. There were many nights where I had to turn on the TV or expected my daughter to entertain herself while I studied and did homework. I was fortunate that God had blessed me with a quiet child who knew how to entertain herself. This helped immensely while trying to get through my studies.

With the help and support of my family and boyfriend, I graduated with my college degree in radiology, along the way making some lifelong friendships. Again, I felt a feeling of accomplishment. I quickly was offered a full-time job at a very good wage. I would be able to support my daughter and myself on my own. I was proud to be able to pick up the phone and cancel all assistance I had been receiving since my daughter's birth. When I did, the lady on the other end said to me, "Honey, that is great, I am very proud of you." Those words brought about a confidence in me, and I will never forget them. I would be able to support my daughter and myself on my own. A year later my boyfriend graduated from the university he was attending with his Bachelor's degree in Computer Science, and moved home.

After dating four and a half years, we became husband and wife. My daughter was six years old. I had the wedding I had always dreamed of with my daughter by my side as my flower girl. That day was one of the best days of my life! I gained an amazing partner and an incredible stepfather for my daughter.

We are both very successful in our chosen careers. We have added two boys to our family since we walked down the aisle. Life is busy. My daughter's father is and has always been a part of her life. She enjoys her time with him, and this I am thankful for. It is not always easy raising a child with two different households and two sets of rules, but it can work, and it does. Our daughter is very well rounded, respectful, a good student, and a very good kid. She loves both of her

Obstacles in your life only make you stronger.

families, which she continues to display in her actions. This is reassurance that we must be doing something right. She is now a senior in high school and balances school, dance team, a job, and family. I feel very fortunate that she is able to have experiences that I didn't have. I could not ask *for a better life* than I have today.

Obstacles in your life only make you stronger. It is how you decide to tackle the obstacle at hand that matters. If you believe in something and have enough determination, you can make it a reality.

As a mom I would do anything for my children. I know my mom tried, did her best, and fought for me to have *a better life*. However, I thought I knew what was best. I was also raised in a Christian home, was taught about a loving God, yet I turned to boys, marijuana, and friends to fill a void in my heart. God wanted me to have *a better life* too, but I had free will and I fought against anything that wanted to control my life. Even though it was all in my best interest, I wanted to be in control!

I have a different mindset now. I have an incredible daughter, two incredible sons, and an amazing husband who loves me unconditionally. I have learned to let God, who never left my side, fill any and every void in my life. I have given Him control. I know when I follow the plans He has for me I will have *a better life*.

"For I know the plans I have for you," declares the LORD, "plans to prosper you and not to harm you, plans to give you hope and a future.
                                                    —Jeremiah 29:11 (NIV)

FORGETTABLE

THE BOWLING BALL of no return dropped deep into the pit of my heart with a startling slam that night. We had set our standards and then compromised them carelessly in the moment. It was hard to not give in to feelings when I knew my

I was so hungry for affection.

boyfriend loved me, I loved him, and I was so hungry for affection. I wasn't sure I was even lovable, but he was certain. The certainty in him felt stable, comforting, and secure to me and I never wanted to let him go.

My life growing up wasn't extreme. We were a Christian middle-class family and I was the middle of three daughters. Being in between two sisters that seemed to shine more brightly than I did, having parents that held attention-demanding leadership positions, and being the recipient of leftovers and hand-me-downs, I felt *forgettable*.

I remember feeling like an afterthought. There was a specific point of determining in my mind to gain approval by overcompensating through performance academically, athletics, and with the opinions of people. I saw when I performed well, I gained the accolades of people who otherwise didn't often verbalize praise. There was an unintentional deficit of affection that grew in my heart and I frantically looked everywhere to fill it up. It only grew deeper and deeper the more I tried to appease this approval addiction.

My own level of self-worth became so low that I sabotaged any attempt of my family to show me love. I became driven, angry, and hardened on the outside; while inside I remained desperate and insecure. By the time I was in high school, I pretended to be a troublemaker to gain attention even though I was too scared to actually be a bad girl, so I dabbled. I would try on the persona while not really wanting to be that person on the inside. I would shoplift once in a while, trying to cover up my misery in cute clothes. Sometimes I would scratch angry words into my arms. Occasionally I would halfway smoke cigarettes at lunch with the partiers, but wouldn't inhale the smoke because I was an "athlete." I'd sneak out after everyone was asleep at night or lie about babysitting jobs to go to parties and drink even though I hated beer. Those parties would always put me in questionable circumstances and box me into choices that threatened my safety. I even pretended to be on drugs just to gain attention from family and friends. I became the anomaly of the family because that's how I viewed myself. I figured sympathy and the drama of negative attention was more exciting than being average and *forgettable*.

Then I met a boy.

This boy was different; he was wise and mature beyond his years because of a painful childhood. He said he loved me and truly meant it. But those words made me extremely angry. How could he love me? That's not possible! We started dating, and from the very first date I knew this was no ordinary date. I had a revelation that it was the beginning of something that would last a lifetime and it scared me to death.

I didn't treat him very well. I had a cold, snippy, and rude attitude. I played hard to get. *We'll just see how much you really love me when you see the "real" me.* I did my usual pattern of sabotaging relationships that offered any love. Yet he pursued and stayed true to his word. I wanted the security of knowing that the worst of me could be loved too. I slowly opened my heart.

As my heart softened, and I stopped pushing affection away, the love of Jesus became more real as well. I had grown up in a Christian church, totally saturated in it, and knew all about Jesus with my head, knew Bible scriptures and stories, and prayed the sinner's prayer because that's what you do. It was robotic.

There came a time though, at about age sixteen, when I had a dream and it shook me up so deeply that I realized I had zero ownership of my relationship with God. I assumed because my parents were Christians and I went to church and I believed God existed, I was peachy. It was a very brief apocalyptic type of dream, maybe just a few minutes long. It didn't need to be any longer than that. It was so vivid and piercing. I remember it clearly to this day, and I don't normally remember my dreams.

I remember these details of the dream: It was a dark moonless night. I had fallen asleep in the bed of a friend's two-wheel-drive pickup truck. He was a good friend in my youth group and like a big brother to me. I woke up suddenly in my dream, to find that I was completely and utterly alone. I was the only one on earth and while I slept, all my friends and family had been taken to heaven. No one told me this—I just knew. At the same time, I looked all around me, then up to the sky and I immediately felt the cold dark realization of complete separation from God that couldn't be reversed. I dropped in anguish and fell apart.

I woke up in real life panic, ran to my youth pastor's house without a second thought and made Jesus Lord of my life. No more lip service or Band-Aid religion. It was a permanent surrender of my heart that I gladly made. I didn't ever want a life without Him again. You can be in the same room with someone all your life and never really know them. I was completely changed, and my boyfriend was forced to hear all about it. He had been going to the same youth group with me before—but when he saw the real change in my heart, he eventually decided he wanted to go the same direction.

At age seventeen, he made Jesus his Lord and Savior as well. I was awakened spiritually, and very sure of who God was, but I still had the baggage of emotional insecurity that needed to be unlearned with a new mental makeover. I was still defaulting to trying to be a Christian; I didn't quite understand the power of who I was now that Jesus had taken over. Some of my choices weren't made in this new identity of Christ in me.

It had been my boyfriend's birthday that day in February, a day full of celebration, and we were feeling quite grown up at seventeen and

Please God, not pregnant. Let me be anything but pregnant.

eighteen years old. We were invincible and carefree. Consequences weren't on our minds at the time, but they weighed heavily on mine by the end of the night. I knew that I knew that I knew in an unexplainable way. It was so obviously clear to me. Just as I knew the sky was blue, my birthdate, and name, I also knew that I was now pregnant. Or technically that I soon would be since science experts say conception takes between five hours and five days.

The Holy Spirit spoke to me and dropped this knowledge into my heart. It was without rebuke, and without a sharp correction of what I should have done. He just plainly, clearly, and softly let me know the truth of my reality. His whisper would alert my heart to accept what would be the grittiest journey I had ever faced. At the same time, His tenderness and kindness brought me to my knees in surrender to His unfailing love and provision. In a state of shock, all I knew to do was run to His Word. I felt it was an anchor in the swells of the storm rising up within me.

Denial felt really good over the next few weeks. Maybe I heard wrong. Maybe it was just my guilty conscience speaking and I'd get a second chance to be normal again. I just wanted to be a normal, typical seventeen-year-old. *Boring* even sounded fantastically delicious. *Please God, not pregnant. Let me be anything but pregnant.* Every symptom confirmed my dread and taunted me. The hole I wanted to sink into disappeared and the blanket I wanted to hide under kept getting flung to the side. I felt so exposed.

At four weeks I needed to go officially confirm what I already knew but didn't want to face. I made the call to a crisis pregnancy center and never felt so alone and small on the inside. I prayed that I could just move past this moment, that it could just be erasable and completely *forgettable.*

I remember sitting in the room talking to a counselor like a little girl trying to play grown-up. The test results came back definite and undeniable. I wished I could stay there in that room forever. The counselor was sweet, loving, and as encouraging as she could possibly be. I knew that once I left that chair, the office door closed behind me, and I got into my car, I was crossing a threshold and there would be no one that could carry this out but me. No one could rescue me or save me or erase what was. I wanted to prolong that visit as long as possible and stay in my pretend cocoon. I went to a school baseball game with some friends immediately afterwards and tried to pretend like everything was the same as always. I felt like I was wearing a gaudy costume with a neon sign that screamed "stupid screw-up." I knew I would never be a teenage girl again. I had to step into the shoes of a woman, and mother. I felt like I was living someone else's life.

If admitting all that to myself wasn't hard enough, we had to face our parents next. It's one thing to disappoint yourself, but it pierces even deeper when you know you are disappointing someone else and it will in turn affect a lot of other people too. My mom and dad weren't just my parents. My dad was also one of the pastors at our church. Even though both sets of our parents were very loving through it all, this announcement wasn't to stay strictly between us and keep within our four walls. It was a very public process that couldn't be a just-get-through-it-and-move-on situation. There were humiliating congregational announcements, looks, stares, and questions. However, there was also love in the middle of it all as a few key people let us know we could do this victoriously.

I kept things quiet at school. This was our senior year and if I could power through that, I felt like I could keep some sense of dignity. So I told none of my friends or coaches. I painted a forced smile on my face, kept competing in sports, going to class, frequently excusing myself to the restroom to go throw up as needed, and even went to prom. All three of us. I didn't want to be "that poor pathetic girl that ruined her life" everywhere I went. I wanted a place where I could try to go back to how it used to be. Thankfully, I just kind of looked thicker, maybe a bit beefier by the time I graduated. I was about three and a half months pregnant.

After graduation I withdrew from a social life and avoided my friends. I had to make excuses why I didn't have a big next steps college plan while everyone else was giddy with excitement over their futures. I had to try to explain why I turned down a full-ride track scholarship and act like that was what I wanted when in reality, it seemed like funeral after funeral for the dreams I had for my life. I celebrated my eighteenth birthday that summer quietly without a lot of excitement, but somehow I knew I'd make it even if I wasn't sure of the exact steps.

Deciding if I would be able to raise this child or have to give him up for adoption was a serious process that was led by prayer. I felt, and believed, abortion was not an option for me. It was ingrained in me that life was precious, valuable, and divine and I wouldn't even consider abortion as an option. Therefore, I had to come to a place of asking God: "Here I am; all of me; all of my messy situation. What's next? How do I move forward with the cards I have and do the right thing in a hard place?"

My boyfriend and I had always talked about getting married, but he was heading off to college out of state in the next few months. I was unsure of what our future together would look like afterwards. We didn't want to get married simply because there was a child. We wanted the decision to be married solely on us wanting to commit to a lifelong relationship to each other, and be ready for that commitment with no regrets. Even in all this uncertainty, I decided pretty quickly I wanted this child with all my heart and it didn't really matter to me if it was hard. I would make it work. I would beat the odds. I would be the best mom I could to him. The thought of someone else being a mom to him ripped my heart out, so I prayed God would help me be all that this little baby boy needed and that he would thrive in knowing how much he was loved even though we were still "babies" ourselves.

Our son was born that November. I was so scared to go through labor, but was really even more scared about if I was able to be a good mom afterwards. The bigger picture of motherhood shadowed the anxiety of labor. Eighteen years old and going through childbirth is a pretty traumatic slap of reality that couldn't be avoided at that point. It was at the time of delivery and meeting his handsome and perfectly made son, that my boyfriend knew he had to lay down his plans to move away and instead be a wholehearted dad. On the outside, he was letting go of something intensely important to him. Thankfully, God moved on his heart with an even more intense desire to pour that focus into making his son the best he could be.

Only God could have done that in the heart of an eighteen-year-old boy, becoming a man. That's not the normal "do what's best for you" philosophy of the world, but it is what parenting is all about. It's a gift of nurturing, providing, and lifting up another person first before yourself, in order to see their life be even better than yours. God does that for us all the time. And I see Him weaving that same desire into us.

Being teenage parents forced us to grow up rapidly, but we took on the challenge knowing that God is our strength. It was embarrassing when people thought I was my son's sister going to parent teacher conferences, and often it seemed they judged our ability. Not surprisingly, we were labeled as "sure to fail" by some. We also had to overcome the feeling of needing to prove ourselves and make up for mistakes. That was a process, but eventually we saw that God always loved us first, by choice.

God loves us wholeheartedly, regardless of our reciprocating that love or our imperfect report card in life. We learned to trust God's Word to provide our every need as we fought against the assumption that being teenage parents meant a life of poverty. God has always provided for us. Sometimes very creatively and just in the knick of time, but He has always seen to it that we were safe, clothed, fed, and had a home and transportation. We never had to use government assistance, but we did have family that helped fill in the gaps when it was needed or when checks bounced from not understanding how to balance a checking account. We worked diligently to do whatever necessary through hard work and sacrifice to get ahead. I'm in awe that God is always upgrading and outdoing Himself in generosity as we've learned to believe and trust Him for more.

I lived with my parents until we married, and worked as a secretary at a furniture store. An amazing foundation for teens with children helped open the door to that job and it made me feel productive and responsible. I remember the heartbreak of leaving our son with a daycare provider when he was six weeks old, but it was necessary if we were going to have long-term victory. With the help of my parents, I was able to go to college and graduated with a

> Being teenage parents forced us to grow up rapidly

> Trust God with your life and your heart. He will remold your dreams into an upgrade you never knew was possible.

Bachelor's degree in Radiology while my husband valiantly worked his way through every door God opened in upper retail management.

It was many strenuous hours for both of us but we were resolute in deciding that we were going to win in life.

We married in the right timing and maturity when we were ready to invest in our relationship together, not trying to fix our past, just ready to create our future. Our parents agreed and I think were even pleased that we had the clarity of mind to take things one step at a time. We've always had a fight in our heart to never quit, always move forward, and let God lead us in His power and wisdom.

Our son is now twenty-three years old, about to marry the woman he loves deeply, preaching God's Word with power every time he gets a chance, and has blessed our lives with his irreplaceable life. We've also been blessed with two more amazing kids and twenty-two years of marriage. We have a non-perfect yet thriving life physically, spiritually, and financially. Our life is better than I ever imagined it would be. I've let go of trying to have the perfect life. That's all a pretend/never good enough standard that can never be attained. I do believe that all Christ is, so are we in this world. Therefore, we should have an extraordinary, prosperous life that overflows with God's endless goodness in every way possible. Everything that felt like loss and defeat before, is really insignificant compared to the gift of unlimited love and supernatural grace God gives to us daily. Our victory has never been about our strength and ability. It's always been about our willingness to let God show Himself strong on our behalf, and trust Him to be our Hero.

Trust God with your life and your heart. He will remold your dreams into an upgrade you never knew was possible. He told me this once and so now I'll tell you the same: "This is not the end of your story. It's just the beginning of something new and different." He has a plan. It's not just a plan to squeak by or barely make it. It's a plan interlaced with

His elements of loving surprises to make you flourish. The details of the surprises He unfolds will be unique and personal to each of us. What you might think is terrible, He wants to transform into terrific. Yield to it and accept His terrific. You'll never regret it.

Through brokenness, bad decisions, and every circumstance, God saw me and held me. He sees you and loves you too. You are the daughter of a King! You are absolutely and completely *un-forgettable!*

> *See what great love the Father has lavished on us, that we should be called children of God! And that is what we are!*
>
> —1 John 3:1 (NIV)

THE MOUNTAIN

I'VE GROWN UP loving mountains. They are majestic and beautiful and they feed my love of camping and hiking. Yet lately, something about that them has felt different. There is a burning in my spirit and tears begin to flow when I look at them. Recently, God has been using mountains as a symbol of my journey from a teen mom to a mature mom. It's a whole new perspective.

Climb the mountain with me...

I recently moved to Redmond, Oregon, where I am surrounded by mountains. Oftentimes, I climb the hill behind our home to take in the splendor of our local mountains: Mt. Bachelor, Broken Top, South Sister "Charity," Middle Sister "Hope," North Sister "Faith," Black Crater, Mount Washington, Three Finger Jack, Black Butte, Mount Jefferson, and Mount Hood. The view is magnificent and watching a sunset from this spot is breathtaking.

During a recent climb, one mountain in particular, South Sister, stood out to me. I didn't know why. My next trip, I brought my journal and asked God to show me why I was so drawn to her. I heard the words *majestic, set apart,* and *beautiful.* These words were not just meant for the mountain, but I felt God saying those words about me, as well.

I developed a yearning deep inside to climb to the top of South Sister. The urgency I felt was overwhelming. I found myself packing a bag and heading out the door the next morning. Climbing South Sister is difficult. The trail to the top of the mountain has a staggering 4,900-foot elevation gain in approximately 6 miles to the 10,358 foot-high peak.

Fear swept through me as I thought about all of the unknowns. I felt unprepared and unsure I could summit.

As I processed these thoughts, I was taken back to how I felt sixteen years ago when I found out I was pregnant with twins. Back then, I found the strength to embrace my fear and overcome the adversity. I felt empowered to walk out that journey up the mountain and allow God to speak to me along the way.

Then God revealed something important to me. He told me I didn't have to make this hike alone to understand what He wanted to teach me. I was reminded that not only did God walk with me in every season of my life, but He also strategically placed people in my path who would encourage me, strengthen me, and give me tools that would empower me to keep going.

One of my dearest friends agreed to join me for the adventure of hiking to the top of South Sister. My heart was racing as we drove toward the mountain. The thought of having to start out at Devil's Lake Trailhead made my stomach turn a little, too.

Interestingly, the closer we got to the trailhead, the more South Sister disappeared from view.

The Path

Arriving at the trailhead, the view was much different from the view I had at home. All we could see was a well-worn path disappearing into the trees. I had to trust this trail was the one that would take me to the top of the mountain, a mountain I couldn't even see anymore.

Stepping out in faith and walking into the unknown also reminded me of how I felt the day I found out I was pregnant.

Even though the path was very well traveled, it definitely was not clear of obstacles. Around every turn there seemed to be a camouflaged rock or tree root, just waiting to trip an unsuspecting hiker. Some were big enough to see clearly, and walk around or step over, but some were small and I would stumble if I wasn't paying attention.

While none of them caught me off guard enough to make me fall, their presence kept me awake and aware. And they made me think back…

As a teen mom, you will likely stumble more than once. Stay focused and learn something each time you fall. Don't turn back just because the path isn't easy; use it as an opportunity to grow stronger.

Less than half a mile into my climb, I started to wonder if I had overpacked. My back was already sore and I was breathing heavy from the uphill climb. We had to take our packs off and find a few minutes of relief from the heavy weight tugging on our shoulders.

In another symbolic way, I was reminded of the heavy burden I carried when I found out I was pregnant. I remembered how I felt: abandoned, angry, afraid, and frustrated. Back then, I could have chosen to end my pregnancy and tell no one. But I chose what at the time felt like the more difficult thing, and *kept going.*

Just like climbing this mountain, I could turn back right now and no one would know.

No one, but me.

After a short break and time to reflect, I put my heavy bag back on and continued putting one foot in front of the other.

In another mile, we once again felt burdened by the weight of our packs and found it difficult to keep going. We hadn't progressed very far and our minds seemed to tell us what we were trying to accomplish was impossible. Our bodies begged us to turn around.

It's in these moments when God calls us to rest in Him so He can comfort, encourage, and reenergize.

I noticed that off to the left of the trail was the perfect log that seemed to say, "It's okay, come rest here." With much relief, we removed the heaviness that weighed down our shoulders and took a moment to sit and listen.

God's beauty was everywhere and we began to recognize His gifts all around us. The trees to the right seemed to create a perfect frame around the peak of another mountain in the distance. There was soothing and comfort as we sat and enjoyed everything around us. I was flooded with excitement as I looked up and saw the mountain, right in front of me.

Until now, we'd been surrounded by forest, which was blocking the view of this majestic mountain.

The mountain didn't move. I just needed to take a moment and slow down long enough to look up so I could see where I was headed.

As a teenager raising a baby, it's not easy to stop and rest, because in most cases you're in survival mode, often having dual roles as mom and dad, while taking care of yourself too. It is crucial you take time to rest and let God fill you up when your tank feels empty. Don't forget to look up. So often, when faced with a difficult situation, the focus remains on where we are, instead of looking up to see where we are headed. Focus your mind on the beauty that will be at the top of your mountain and push through the adversity, exhaustion, and pain.

With the top of South Sister finally in sight, I began to realize the hardest part was yet to come. I wondered if I had what it would take to make it. The signs up ahead gave me three options.

Option one: I could turn back, and give into my exhaustion, hurting feet, and aching shoulders.

Option two: I could take the detour downhill to Moraine Lake, stay in my comfort zone, and enjoy the beauty there.

Option three: I could walk in obedience to what God called me to do and rely on Him and His strength to push through to the summit.

Although the detour would allow me to take in more of God's beautiful creation, I knew that was not what He wanted. God is patient. He allows us to walk off-course because of our free will. I knew if I took that route, He would patiently wait for me to get back on the path He instructed me to take. If I chose to wander off the path I was meant to be on, I would at some point have to make the climb back up to this same intersection and continue on His path. I knew the path He wanted me to take was the trail to the top.

After catching my breath, drinking some water, and eating a snack, I was refueled and ready to press on. I was grateful for that moment of rest and a glimpse of where I was headed.

The path continued flat and wide for a while. I enjoyed being able to move forward without my lungs having to work so hard. I was able to enjoy the beauty around me since I no longer had to worry so much about stumbling over rocks and roots. My friend and I were even able to enjoy a wonderful conversation.

But I also knew the journey wasn't over yet.

· Just as in life, the path began to narrow and the difficulty increased again. It was obvious that not as many people made it to this part of the trail. A few times the path split in two different directions and we would stop and ask, "Which trail, God?" We had to trust we were continuing on the path He wanted for us.

We knew that no matter what path we chose, as long as we were moving toward the top of the mountain, we were walking in obedience to what He asked us to do.

Then we noticed that every time the path seemed to split, and we had to decide which one to follow, they always joined back together with the main path leading to the top of the mountain. I realized then that God was saying to me, "Daughter, which path do you want to take? You are walking in the direction I asked you to and I will be with you no matter which direction you choose."

As the path got more difficult, I doubted my ability to overcome the pain I felt consuming me. Several people offered encouragement on their way down the mountain. They offered hope that it could be done. Their faces were filled with joy because of what they had seen at the top and they told us how close we were.

Their hope helped us push through the pain. The loose rocks under my feet made it feel like I was getting nowhere. With every step forward, I felt myself slip backward. I knew that even if they were only baby steps, I was still making progress and that was enough to keep me going. I kept the top of the mountain in my sights. *I can do this! Fill me up, God!*

As I climbed, I thought about those situations as a teen mom when I felt like a step forward was impossible. Yet in those moments, God sent people to encourage me along the way. After awhile, I knew to look for them. They were truly a gift from Him who can bring strength when it feels too difficult to press forward.

The False Summit

In mountain climbing, a false summit is a peak that appears to be the top of the mountain, but isn't. Reaching the "false summit" that day felt incredible. The view was beautiful and it felt like we had done enough to feel successful. Getting to that place was an amazing accomplishment! However, no matter how comfortable we felt at that point, I knew our journey was not over and it was going to get even harder. This path was even less traveled.

The false summit experience reminded me of when I decided I no longer wanted to work three jobs to make ends meet and live off state assistance. I was comfortable. My twins and I had a place of our own, and were not going without. Yet I wanted more and knew I had to keep going no matter how hard it would be. God called me higher!

That day on South Sister, my friend and I felt like we had just pressed through something so difficult we couldn't bear to face another section of the trail that was equally tough to climb. People coming down the mountain warned us the trail ahead was ten times worse than what we already walked through. In spite of their warnings, we knew we had to push forward and face the treacherous red rock. We couldn't stop short of our destination.

It seemed impossible to get a foothold. My shoes weren't made for hiking and had no traction on the bottom. With every step, I found myself sliding backwards. My friend was several steps in front of me, and equally exhausted, but she would still offer a thumbs-up, encouraging me whenever our eyes met.

We were so close to the top, yet it felt so far away. Every part of my body ached; I began to wonder if my steps really got me anywhere, and if I really had what it took to make it to the top. I began to question if it was really worth all the pain. I stopped several times along the way to look back and see how far I had already come. Each time it gave me a little more energy to take one more step towards the summit.

I began to speak God's truth in my mind. "With God, all things are possible. I can do all things through Christ who strengthens me." This created a shift inside of me to pray boldly and ask God not to make the path easier, but that He would strengthen me instead.

I reflected back to the beginning of the hike when boulders and tree roots felt like obstacles in my way. However, during this part of the climb as my feet continued slipping and couldn't seem to move me forward, I was grateful for the boulders and even prayed for them. This allowed my arms and feet to work together, moving my body forward. I needed something to hang on to and the boulders became a solid support.

God reminded me then, that the hard stuff in life, "the boulders in your path," are not always obstacles intended to make you fall, but are placed strategically along your path when you need them. He went before me and prepared the way, not making it easier, but providing the strength I needed to ascend to the top.

The Journey

We did it! We reached the summit! We had overcome exhaustion, fought through pain, and continued our climb even when it was difficult. The wind blew fiercely and we found comfort and refuge in the rock forts built on top, a place to catch our breath and empty rocks out of our shoes.

This time our rest was short, because we were so overwhelmed with excitement at what we'd accomplished. This place gave us rest and hid us from the wind, but it also blocked our view of the beauty surrounding us. We had to get out of this place of temporary comfort once again and walk the short distance to the "true summit," which was not much further and an easy walk.

That was the view we came for.

But now the wind was so cold. The blanket of snow was beautiful and untouched except for a path across the middle. As we walked along the path, God gave me an image of Him walking with me. I was a little girl and He was holding my hand and smiling down at me saying, "Walk with Me daughter, I have something to show you." I was skipping because I was so excited to see what He had in store! This vision renewed my entire body and I began to giggle with joy. All despair was forgotten and I could no longer feel the pain.

This walk of obedience up the mountain was not easy, but God was about to show me that even though it wasn't easy, it was worth it!

The view from the top was incredible. I was able to see the mountains around us from a completely new perspective. Each one was beautiful. Each with its own story. Yet I couldn't see the path someone might have had to walk or the things he or she might have had to face along the way to get there.

As a teen mom, you might find yourself in a similar place. You might be comparing your journey to someone else's. While the difficulties you face are still fresh in your mind, you might wish you could have climbed someone else's mountain. One that appears easier, smaller, less cluttered with obstacles, and one you might think would have a better view.

You may look at another teen mom who seems to have it all together, but you have no idea what it took for her to make it to that place in her journey. God went before you, chose you, and prepared the way for you. Whatever it is you face, this is your mountain and only you can climb it.

That day, I looked back once again at the path we'd traveled, and suddenly it didn't seem difficult. From this vantage point, all that could be seen was beauty. I began to reflect on everything placed in my path to get me there. The view from the top was incredible, but power and strength were built in the journey.

I started along the path thinking it was all about getting to the top, but I learned so much along the way. God never left my side and He provided for my needs in every step. He went before me and set out places to rest when I felt weak, created a soft breeze that reminded me He was near, and provided beauty to keep me walking into the unknown. He provided encouragement as He placed people along the path when I began to feel weak, and a friend to walk alongside me to motivate each other when one of us didn't feel strong enough to take another step.

Somehow, in the times I needed it most, the things I needed were there when I pressed forward using a power that was not my own. It was just enough to strengthen me to take another step.

As much as we wanted to remain at the top, we knew we needed to start the journey back to the car before darkness set in. Our body aches were no longer masked by the excitement of reaching the top. My legs were shaking and I would have given anything to stay in my place of comfort at the top. I'd made the journey, hadn't I? Yet I knew I would die if I tried to stay there. We didn't have enough food or shelter, and the weather at the mountaintop can change at a moment's notice. *God didn't bring me here to stay comfortable,* I realized.

power and strength were built in the journey.

He gave me just enough to make the journey. It's truly amazing what your body is capable of when you have no other choice.

As a teen mom you are suddenly able to survive with very little sleep, work extremely hard, overcome whatever is thrown at you simply because you have no other options—all because you have a baby who is counting on you to overcome adversity. You have the ability to slip into survival mode and find a strength you didn't know existed. You do it when you are afraid, when it's difficult, and when you are tired.

Regardless of the exhaustion we felt, my friend and I had to make the journey back down.

We ended up hiking the last couple of miles in the dark.

As we arrived at the trailhead late in the evening, exhausted, sore, and relieved to have completed our journey, we realized we'd lost the car keys somewhere on the hike! With only a couple bars of battery left on my phone, we called for help.

We knew then why we'd packed such heavy bags. God once again had walked before us and prepared the way. He knew the struggle we would face. I was new to the area and my friend would only be staying in Bend for the summer. Yet months ahead of this journey, He placed friends in our path who had willing hearts to help. Friends willing to jump out of bed and drive an hour to rescue us and friends who stayed up praying for us until they knew we were safe. It felt like we had over-packed but we had jackets and extra food too.

God protected us once again.

Listen:

You may feel like you have just been dropped off at the bottom of your mountain.

The trail may appear impossible, the journey unknown.

There will be boulders that will try to knock you off-track, boulders of shame, doubt, ridicule, and hopelessness.

There will be times when you feel like there is no way you will ever make it.

There will be times when you feel off-balance, stumble, and fall.

There will be days when you have trouble catching your breath from feeling overwhelmed.

> Your testimony
> could be the
> key that unlocks
> someone else's
> prison.

The journey of a teen mom is not easy. But remember that many others have walked this path before you. They can show you things, so you don't make the same mistakes they did. Life isn't easy, but if you use the wisdom of those who have gone before you, it can save you so much heartache. Their journeys, their insight, and their wisdom can bring you comfort during the storms you face. Strength will come when you need it, and your journey will serve to create a clearer path for others to follow.

The top of the mountain provides a whole new perspective. No longer are you only able to see that which is directly in front of you. From the summit, you can look back and see the path you took. You can see beauty everywhere, and praise God for walking alongside you and keeping you safe.

Once you have seen the top of the mountain, a whole new journey begins as you head back down. As you descend the path, you are able to encourage others who are still fighting to get to the top.

You're also able to encourage those at the bottom who are afraid to take the first step. Before you realize it, your story will offer hope to others.

Be an overcomer, face adversity head on, be victorious! But don't stay there. Eventually you will be called to lead. Share your story and the obstacles you faced along the way. Your testimony could be the key that unlocks someone else's prison. It will empower them to step out and say "I can do it too." So don't be afraid to share what you walked through.

Then one day, you'll get to see the same mountain from yet another perspective. From miles away, the path you traveled can no longer be seen. From this perspective, there is no more fear. From this distance, all you see is the majestic beauty in every mountain, including your own. Each of them so very different, yet each perfectly created.

I pray one day you will look back and see the beauty in your journey and in your mountain.

You are not alone as you climb the mountain. God is with you along the path. He will guide you past the false summit, and encourage you on the journey. All God asks is that you take the first step.

This is your *starting point*!

WHAT NEXT?

HAS IT BEEN on your heart to mentor a teen mom? Are you a teen mom looking for a mentor?

This book is simply the Starting Point to a ministry that will continue to be a support to teen moms. You can be part of this journey by contacting us at...

https://www.facebook.com/ThisIsYourStartingPoint/
or E-mail ThisIsYourStartingPoint@aol.com

May God bless you always!
—*Tiffany Stadler*

CONTACT INFORMATION

REDEMPTION
PRESS

To order additional copies of this book, please visit
www.redemption-press.com.
Also available on Amazon.com and BarnesandNoble.com
Or by calling toll free 1-844-2REDEEM.

CPSIA information can be obtained
at www.ICGtesting.com
Printed in the USA
FFOW01n1752080417
34352FF